DISASTERS:

Mental Health Interventions

John D. Weaver, LSW, ACSW

CRISIS MANAGEMENT SERIES

Series Editors:
Frank M. Dattilio, PhD and Arthur Freeman, EdD

Professional Resource Press
Sarasota, Florida

Published by Professional Resource Press
(An imprint of Professional Resource Exchange, Inc.)
Post Office Box 15560
Sarasota, FL 34277-1560

Some of the photos appearing on the cover were provided by permission of the American Red Cross.

The copy editor for this book was Patricia Hammond, the managing editor was Debra Fink, the production coordinator was Laurie Girsch, and Jami's Graphic Design created the cover.

Library of Congress Cataloging-in-Publication Data

Weaver, John D., date.
    Disasters : mental health interventions / John D. Weaver.
        p.   cm. -- (Crisis management series)
    Includes bibliographical references and index.
    ISBN 1-56887-011-6
    1. Disaster victims--Mental health services. 2. Crisis
intervention (Psychiatry) 3. Disasters--Psychological aspects.
4. Post-traumatic stress disorder. I. Title. II. Series.
RC451.4.D57W43   1995
616.85′21--dc20   95-3891
                                                   CIP

ABOUT THE AUTHOR

John D. Weaver, MSW, ACSW, is a licensed clinical social worker currently serving as Casework Supervisor for Northampton County Mental Health and as a part-time therapist with Concern, an outpatient mental health clinic, both in Bethlehem, Pennsylvania. Mr. Weaver has served as a member of the adjunct faculties of Marywood College School of Social Work, Lehigh Valley Campus, and of the Northampton Community College, Bethlehem. He also maintains a private consulting practice specializing in mental health and crisis intervention services and risk management related training.

Mr. Weaver received his Master's Degree in Social Work from the University of Pennsylvania. He has written several articles and one earlier book, *An Untapped Resource: Working With Volunteers Who Are Mentally Ill* (MBA Publishing) Throughout his career, he has been an active volunteer with the American Red Cross and has assisted at several local and national disasters including the Mississippi River/Midwest floods of 1993, and the 1994 crash of USAir Flight 427.

DEDICATION

To my wife, Denise, and my two children, Scott and Kelly, who have always been extremely tolerant of the time I have spent on the road as a disaster mental health volunteer. Their enduring patience was further tested, and, again, they were very supportive, as I spent several months at my computer working on this book.

ABSTRACT

Tropical storms, tornadoes, fires, floods, earthquakes, airplane crashes (and other transportation accidents), hazardous material spills, building collapses, nuclear plant malfunctions, terrorist bombings, mud slides, and many other disasters occur throughout our country each year. In the wake of these disasters lies a wide path of physical and psychological destruction. Many seriously traumatized people can be found there, struggling to recover from their losses and rebuild their homes and their lives.

Disaster mental health (DMH) is a growing field of practice designed to help the victims, and the helpers who rush to their aid, learn to cope effectively with the extreme stresses they will face in the aftermath of a disaster. This volume will provide a practical overview of the DMH field and the many opportunities it offers to those who are willing and able to assist others in times of disaster.

Significant background literature is reviewed, with emphasis on material published by the Center for Mental Health Services (CMHS), formerly called the National Institute of Mental Health (NIMH). Sections cover subjects including crisis intervention, screening, support, consultation, preparedness planning, bereavement, supervision, working with the media, Post-Traumatic Stress Disorder (PTSD), burnout, and survival techniques relevant to both victims and helpers. Information is presented via a blend of references to relevant literature and personal observations made during the author's experiences on national assignments with the American Red Cross. Readers are challenged to become involved with this passionately addictive field of practice.

TABLE OF CONTENTS

DISASTERS:

Mental Health Interventions

INTRODUCTION

Tropical storms, tornadoes, fires, floods, earthquakes, plane crashes (or other transportation accidents), hazardous material spills, terrorist bombings, volcanic eruptions, building collapses, nuclear plant malfunctions, mud slides, ice storms, blizzards, and any number of other natural, accidental, or intentionally inflicted disasters strike throughout our country each year. These events range in scope from small, single-home fires, to large, catastrophic natural phenomena, such as 1989's Loma Prieta (San Francisco Bay Area) earthquake, 1992's Hurricane Andrew, 1993's Mississippi River/Midwest floods, and 1994's Los Angeles earthquake.

In the wake of these disasters lies a path of physical destruction, property loss, serious injuries, and deaths to persons who happened to be in the affected area at the time when the disaster struck. Also in the disaster's wake, less obvious to an untrained observer, is a path of emotional destruction as people struggle to rebuild their lives while living with the traumatic memories of what has just occurred.

Reestablishing communication, assessing the damage, cleaning up the mess, and reconstructing the homes and businesses is costly and time consuming. Nevertheless, it is often the easier part of the process of getting things back to normal. The harder part for many disaster victims is assessing the emotional damage that can be caused by an event this stressful and effectively expressing or venting the array of emotional responses that will surface during the recovery process.

The ultimate goal of disaster mental health (DMH) is to lessen the likelihood that negative, long-term mental health problems, such as Post-Traumatic Stress Disorders (PTSDs), will occur as a result of the incidents. To do this, DMH workers utilize a vast array of approaches, including emotional first aid; crisis intervention; defusing and debriefing; consultation with local agencies, schools, and community caregivers; public education via broadcast and print media; brief supportive counseling; and

screening and referral for those who are experiencing more serious difficulties.

This volume will provide the reader with a practical overview of the DMH field and the many opportunities it offers to
those who are willing and able to assist others in times of disaster. Significant background literature will be reviewed, with
special emphasis on material published by the Center for Mental Health Services (CMHS), formerly called the National Institute of Mental Health (NIMH).* Crisis intervention (CI), screening, support, and survival techniques, suitable for both victims
and helpers, will be presented using a combination of references
to relevant literature and personal observations made during
experiences that I have had while working locally or on national
assignments with the American Red Cross (ARC) Disaster Services Human Resources (DSHR) System.

In writing this book, I have tried to provide those readers
who have already been serving in disaster relief operations, either as DMH workers or as representatives of the many other
areas of specialization, with the kinds of material that will help
them learn (or rediscover):

1. Information about the historical and philosophical un-
   derpinnings of DMH work.
2. Factors that distinguish a disaster from a crisis situation.
3. Typical and atypical responses to disasters, plus insights
   into the context of disaster response, including information about the roles played by government agencies/of-
   ficials and how they interface with ARC and many other
   relief organizations.
4. Basic screening and intervention methods for use with
   victims and helpers.

---

*As this book was going to press, the name of the National Institute of
Mental Health (NIMH) was changed to the Center for Mental Health
Services (CMHS). Publications by NIMH/CMHS can be obtained from
the Office of Consumer, Family, and Public Information, Center for Mental
Health Services, 5600 Fishers Lane, Room #13-103, Rockville, MD 20857;
telephone (301) 443-2792. The Emergency Services and Disaster Relief
Branch of CMHS can be contacted at 5600 Fishers Lane, Room #16C-26,
Rockville, MD 20857; telephone (301) 443-4735.

5. Advice on how DMH workers can learn to monitor and handle their own stress (and that of their coworkers).
6. A brief overview of issues relating to planning and supervising a DMH operation.
7. Potential areas for future involvement in some aspects of DMH-related practice that are different from those they have already experienced.

If I have done my job properly, the practical information and techniques that are summarized in the coming pages will help the experienced reader with future assignments.

My greater hope, however, is that this volume will capture the interest of persons who may have thought about DMH, or other types of relief work, but have not yet taken any steps to become involved. Without a doubt, most readers who fall into the category of "interested but not yet involved" need only go out on one assignment to become hooked, as happened with me and with several of the new friends whom I have met through DMH trips.

Chapter 1

ANATOMY OF A CRISIS

Before moving into the sections of this book that provide detailed information about DMH history, philosophy, and techniques, it seems appropriate to briefly review some basic material about crises and disasters. These definitions and concepts can then serve as a common foundation for the remainder of the book.

Crisis intervention (CI) has been defined by Parad et al. (1975a) as:

> the active entering into the life situation of an individual, family, or group to: (1) cushion the impact of a stress that throws the person (or persons) off balance and (2) help mobilize the resources of those affected directly by the stress. (p. 5)

To Parad and his coauthors, a crisis consists of four critically integral elements:

1. a *precipitating event* (or stressor);
2. *perception of the event;*
3. *response to the event;* and,
4. *resolution* of the problem(s). (pp. 6-7)

These fit nicely with any discussion of DMH.

Just about anything that happens to us can be considered a *precipitating event* (or stressor). Life presents each of us with a constant supply of events. Some of them prove to be beneficial, while others result in the kinds of dubious consequences that we would have preferred to avoid. Births and deaths, promotions and layoffs, winning and losing, growing up and growing old — all are a part of the fabric of life, and any of these can be the start of a crisis in our lives.

Perception of the event, how each of us views the mix of routine and bizarre life events we face each day, has a great deal to do with how well we eventually resolve the resulting crises. For example, some people see the death of a spouse as a traumatic challenge that they must struggle to overcome; others see it as the end of the road for both partners, and they may soon die themselves, having lost their own will to live.

The *response period* (or crisis state) is a time of emotional difficulty and often pain. Whatever physical and psychological stability existed before the crisis occurred may now be greatly altered or altogether gone. This is a period characterized by trial-and-error efforts at regaining some semblance of order that can facilitate a return to pre-crisis conditions.

The *resolution period* comes when the adaptive coping or problem-solving efforts have fallen into place and serious progress toward recovery is becoming a reality. People can finally see and believe that the immediate goals they have set for themselves are indeed reachable.

Now that a working definition of crisis intervention and a common understanding of what constitutes a crisis has been established, we can now examine how crises are compared to disasters. It is important to keep these four elements in mind as we examine the makeup of a disaster.

Chapter 2

WHAT CONSTITUTES
A DISASTER?

If you were asked, "What is a disaster?" how would you respond? Possibly, you would begin by making some joking remarks about the horrible day you had at work yesterday, your uncontrollable weight, personal finances (or maybe just the way you manage your checkbook and tax records), a worn-out car you are driving, the inveterate messiness of your child's bedroom, or your last golf score.

Then, upon more serious reflection, you would probably begin listing certain named events like Hurricanes Andrew, Iniki, Hugo, or Agnes; the Mississippi River/Midwest flood (or those in Corning or Buffalo Creek); the Loma Prieta or the Los Angeles earthquake; the Oakland Hills fire; the Challenger explosion; the Los Angeles riots; the Three-Mile Island nuclear accident; the eruption of Mt. St. Helens; or the World Trade Center bombing. It is likely that the events that you name will depend upon several factors, including your age, your memory, your proximity to the impacted area, and your relationships with family members and friends who were somehow affected.

As you look at the short list of disasters in the preceding paragraph, or as you think about other, similar occurrences that have touched your life, you will, no doubt, be amazed by how vividly each of us can remember many of these traumatic slices of life. This is probably a testament to how well the graphic images of suffering from every recent, major disaster have been documented and relayed to us by broadcast and print media. But what qualifies these events as disasters?

Quarantelli's perspective in "What Is Disaster . . ." (1985, pp. 41-52) focuses on a combination of seven elements:

1. *Physical agents* (the fires, floods, tornadoes, etc.).

2. *Physical impact* (the visually observable destruction done by the physical agents).
3. *Assessment of physical impacts* (the damage has to exceed certain thresholds).
4. *Social disruption* (due to physical damage).
5. *Social constructions of reality* (perceptions of the seriousness of the impact).
6. *Political definitions* (official disaster declarations).
7. *Demands for action* (which exceed normal response capabilities).

The first three elements are physical dimensions, and the latter four are psychosocial. Quarantelli stresses that disasters must be social occasions. Quite a substantial number of people must be involved, and there must be a public consensus on the elements noted previously, or it will be viewed as just another crisis, rather than a disaster.

In the same essay, Quarantelli (1985, pp. 52-65) reviews eight characteristics of community responses to disasters that greatly influence the number and types of mental health problems the event's victims will experience:

1. *Proportion of population that is directly involved.*
2. *Social centrality of the affected population.*
3. *Length of involvement.*
4. *Rapidity of involvement.*
5. *Predictability of involvement.*
6. *Unfamiliarity* with the crises of a major disaster.
7. *Depth of involvement* (individual losses compared with losses suffered by others in community).
8. *Recurrency of involvement* (e.g., life in a flood-prone area, where every few years there may be problems).

These eight factors usually become the chief determinates of the four psychosocial elements in Quarantelli's definition of disaster. For DMH workers, the emotional fallout from these psychosocial changes becomes the greatest defining concern as they think about the concept of disaster.

Baum and Davidson (1985) note the critical roles that both the *stressors* (the disaster events and related changes in people's lives) and the *appraisal* (individuals' event-related perceptions and responses) play in outcomes. When victims or helpers are unsuccessful in confronting and managing the combination of real and perceived threat, the so-called *stress response* of the body preparing for *fight or flight* is the result. Profound changes occur in both physical and cognitive systems as people strain to cope. If their efforts fail, the potential costs can be high, as a variety of physical and/or mental illnesses may result.

Bolin's (1985) examination of the psychosocial impact of disasters talks about *victim level* and *trauma potential. Primary level victims* are those who directly experience the event and suffer the related, catastrophic losses of life and property. They are the individuals in greatest need of DMH assistance. *Secondary level victims* also witness and experience the event (sometimes doing so from far away, via media coverage) and may have even lost friends or family members, but somehow they have not been so deeply distressed by it. Members of this group usually do not perceive themselves as true victims, and they are far less likely to seek DMH help. A third group, the helpers who serve in relief roles, is also subjected to large amounts of post-disaster stress.

Trauma potential exists, according to Bolin, in several *impact characteristics* that somewhat overlap with Quarantelli's findings. The characteristics Bolin lists are *terror and horror* of the events witnessed and the related losses; *duration of impact; unexpectedness* of the event; *threat* posed (pre-impact perception of risk); *impact ratio* (portion of community suffering losses); *sociocultural changes* during recovery (changes in daily routine and level of control over one's life); *symbolism* of events (human-made events, intentional or due to error, tend to be extremely traumatic); and *interactive and cumulative effects* of these and other pre- and post-disaster issues upon victims and helpers who themselves vary greatly in personality types, pre-disaster emotional state, and ability to manage stress (pp. 3-28). As these features vary from victim to victim, and from one event to the next, so, too, will the emotional impact.

These perspectives are psychosocial definitions of disasters. The next chapter will briefly examine some more material ways to define and classify disaster events. But, before moving into the next section, it may help to convey the essence of disasters if we make matters a bit more personal.

Picture yourself in the situation the survivors are facing. Before the disaster, your life is going along relatively smoothly. You have routine problems, but so does everyone else. You and your family are doing the best you can do with your present homes, jobs, and so on. Then, the unexpected and traumatic event occurs.

Imagine that your neighborhood has just been hit by a severe storm. Several inches of rain have fallen and flash flooding has occurred. You have just arrived home from work and been impacted by the traumatic *insult* which occurred as you discovered what has happened.

Your home has water in it that may only be flooding the basement. What will you lose? (Maybe just some old stuff you never use.) The water may be up 3 feet into the first-floor living area; what has been affected now? (Sofas, chairs, tables, books, televisions and appliances, etc.) What if the water has risen 6 feet? (Pictures, photo albums, clothing, etc.) Now imagine the whole house inundated, right up to the top of the roof line. Think about your potential losses of belongings and related memories.

A few houses up the street, some of the neighbors' homes sat on a hill. There was no damage at all. You have had to relocate, but they are still in their own homes. Why were they so lucky? They have no idea what you and your family are going through!

A few houses in the other direction, a tornado touched down, destroying one home and killing several members of the family that lived there — people whom you knew quite well. That could have been you and your family. At least no one in your family was hurt, and your home may still be standing and repairable.

Your ability to function will likely become diminished for some interval of time following the disaster. It will return gradually as you navigate the bumpy and jagged road to recovery. You will want to make things right immediately, and you will wish things could be like they were before. The length of the recovery period will probably turn out to be far longer than you ever imagined.

With any luck, things will eventually turn out at least as well for you as they were before the disaster. For some people, things will even be better as they incorporate what they have learned about themselves during the emotional journey; they will become stronger individuals. For others, things will not turn out so well. Some will give up or fail under the extreme pressure. Their outcomes will not be nearly as positive.

These are the kinds of things that happen in disasters. Victims' lives are touched in many ways. Some people barely seem to have been affected, while others seem to have been devastated, both physically and emotionally. People's responses will also vary over time, as they move through the various stages of recovery. Dealing with the psychological aftermath of these random destructive events is what DMH is all about.

One of the greatest challenges of DMH comes as workers try to sort out the disaster-related issues from the preexisting stressors and chronic social problems that may have been troubling the residents long before the disaster struck. During the early days following Hurricane Andrew, for instance, communities' problems and needs differed significantly, according to Mays (1993). In Florida, looting was rampant, and local drug gangs with automatic weapons were common hazards. Citizens were armed and afraid to leave their badly damaged homes until various uniformed military and National Guard units blanketed the area, restoring order by their mere presence. Across the Gulf of Mexico, in Louisiana, there were no significant problems with looting or violence. Instead, inadequate, overcrowded housing was the main social concern, as victims squeezed themselves into the less-damaged residences of friends and relatives.

Mays' observations at a 1993 workshop on federal disaster response were shared by other members of the armed forces with whom I spoke during and after that workshop. Mays anticipates that the peacetime military will probably be called upon more and more for domestic relief efforts. As you can imagine, the National Guard presence in Florida following Andrew was invaluable. In keeping with Maslow's hierarchy of needs, until an area's immediate needs for food, shelter, and safety are met, it is virtually impossible to work with the victims on any other DMH recovery issues.

Chapter 3

CLASSIFICATION, DECLARATION, AND SCOPE OF DISASTERS

Unless you already have an interest in disaster relief, you probably do not realize how large and complex a disaster operation can be. This brief section is designed to give readers a background perspective on some ways disasters can be characterized.

AMERICAN RED CROSS (ARC) CLASSIFICATION SYSTEM

Within ARC, each disaster is assigned a classification level based upon estimates of the amount of money that is likely to be expended by ARC during the operation. The DSHR manual (ARC, 1987) lists the classifications as follows:

Level I - recurrent, local disasters
Level II - costs ARC less than $50,000 (excluding recurrent local disaster needs)
Level III - costs ARC from $50,000 to $250,000
Level IV - costs ARC from $250,000 to $2.5 million
Level V - costs to ARC exceed $2.5 million (p.28)

ARC uses the classification levels, together with other specific information about the triggering event, to help assess staffing needs. Based upon previous disaster experiences, those who plan, outline, and implement the organization's disaster responses can tell quite a bit about how many persons are needed from each specialization and what ranks (techs, specialists, etc.) they must hold for various level jobs.

ARC puts out press releases summarizing statistics for the disasters they are working. As an example of the staggering numbers of people ARC serves, and the numbers of workers needed, here are some of the statistics that were provided to me by the public affairs staff regarding just the Iowa and Illinois portion of the Mississippi River/Midwest floods, for my use in contacts with the media while I was on that assignment (ARC, personal communication, August 3, 1993):

    total homes affected 15,000
    ARC service centers open at job peak 21
    ARC shelters open (at peak) .27
    people housed in shelters (at peak) 1,555
    mental health referrals 5,252
    ARC workers on the job (total to date) 2,647
    meals served 319,996
    estimated cost of ARC operation . . . . $3.5 million

It is important to keep in mind that this operation was covering just one section of the vast area that was hit by this great flood. Similar operations were occurring all over the middle portion of the country at that time.

As the publication deadline for this book neared, I checked back with ARC National Headquarters for more current statistics on their work throughout the whole Mississippi River/Midwest flood zone. They provided me with these even more staggering numbers (from a September 10, 1993 press release):

    total homes affected 56,295
    ARC service centers open at job peak 99
    ARC shelters open (at peak) 145
    people housed in shelters (at peak) 14,502
    mental health referrals 28,122
    ARC workers on the job (total to date) 14,536
    meals served 2,517,476
    estimated cost of ARC operation . . . . $30.2 million

Eighty percent of the ARC workers were volunteers, and I am proud to have been one of them. Despite my direct involvement in this massive relief effort, however, I still find myself amazed by how large an operation this was.

FEDERAL DISASTER DECLARATION

Major disasters are *declared* when they exceed the scope that can be handled by local communities or states without additional federal aid. Requests for aid are made by the governors of the affected states to the office of the president. Once the need has been verified, the president signs the declaration. Receiving a declaration qualifies a community for federal help in the form of grants and loans, in the form of relief supplies, and in the use of various facilities and services, including the DMH expertise of the staff members at the Center for Mental Health Services (CMHS).

Where ARC's role is to take care of the immediate personal needs of disaster victims, the government takes primary responsibility for infrastructure (homes, businesses, buildings, roads, etc.), but also helps with individual assistance. Established in 1979, the Federal Emergency Management Agency (FEMA) coordinates the government's relief efforts, provides repair and aid grants, and sometimes provides temporary housing.

FEMA also establishes *Disaster Application Centers* (DACs) where victims can go to get federal aid. Several other federal agencies are also usually involved, including the following:

- *Small Business Administration* — for loans to repair or replace personal property, homes, and small businesses (buildings, equipment, and items lost from inventory)
- *U. S. Department of Agriculture* — for food stamps
- *Farmers Home Administration* — also provides loans for use in repairing or replacing real or personal property
- *Department of Labor* — pays unemployment compensation for persons out of work due to a disaster and can help with finding new employment
- *Internal Revenue Service* — will assist with filing returns that involve disaster-related losses.

FEMA will work with local and state level mental health officials and will even fund special crisis counseling and follow-up treatment services. The money comes into the local area in the form of Immediate Services Grants. Advance planning helps speed the grant process. DMH consultation is often helpful during the process of requesting these grants. Disasters require complex interaction between many branches and levels of government. Those readers interested in knowing more about the relief process might wish to refer to Myers (1994). Her book provides considerable detail about governmental response to disasters.

Various government statistics show that, since 1974, the United States has averaged about 29 disaster declarations per year. During 1992, 45 major disasters were declared, making it the worst year on record for FEMA. Hurricane Andrew, so far the greatest disaster in U.S. history, led with (a) $30 billion dollars in estimated economic losses; (b) 75,000 seriously damaged or destroyed homes (and 8,000 businesses); and (c) 160,000 people left homeless. Federal assistance in excess of $1.8 billion dollars will be spent on the Andrew-related recovery efforts in Florida alone, according to recent figures by the Government Accounting Office (U.S. GAO, 1993).

Andrew was what is known as a *Category 4* hurricane — about as bad as they get. Still, as anyone familiar with southern Florida geography well knows, a course shift of about 20 miles would have squarely hit Miami and probably caused far more extensive (and expensive) property damage and greater loss of life.

How big were some other disasters in terms of federal monies spent on recovery? In preparing this book, I requested recent funding statistics from FEMA. Below is a portion of the information an Emergency Management Specialist from FEMA compiled for me, summarizing the *millions* of relief dollars that his office is projecting will be spent by the United States, once all the bills have been paid, on some of the worst disasters of the past few years:

Disaster	**Amount in Millions**
Hurricane Andrew (1992)	$2,079
Hurricane Hugo (1989)	$1,585
Mississippi/Midwest floods (1993)	$802
Loma Prieta earthquake (1989)	$689
Hurricane Iniki (1992)	$329
Los Angeles riots (1992)	$180

The Mississippi River/Midwest floods of 1993 exceeded Andrew in terms of the land area that was involved, but did not cause the kinds of major damage to infrastructure that resulted from Andrew. Final damage and cost figures are not yet available, but the current projection from FEMA is that it will not exceed Andrew in cost to the federal government (H. Humes, personal communication, October 15, 1993).

MORE GAUGES OF DISASTER

The National Guard has played an important role in several recent disasters. Ward (1993) reported these telling deployment statistics:

Loma Prieta earthquake 16,599
Los Angeles riots 10,000
Mississippi/Midwest floods 8,710
Hurricane Andrew 7,715
Hurricane Iniki 2,177

Guard members occasionally pay the ultimate price for their sometimes dangerous relief role, as did a 30-year-old sergeant who was accidentally killed during the Mississippi/Midwest flood. He was working in Des Moines, trying to set up a communications antenna, when it fell and touched a high-voltage power line. According to friends, he died doing what he did best—he was "helping others" (Ritter, 1993, p. 8A). He was survived by a wife and a 2-year-old daughter.

Sadly, fatality statistics are another way to gauge the scope of disasters. Ritter (1993), who reported the story of the Guardsman, also tells the stories of many of the 46 other casualties of the "Great Flood of '93—victims of freak accidents, unforeseen circumstances, [and] sometimes poor judgement" (p. 8A). Among those lost during the Mississippi/Midwest floods were four young hikers and their two counselors, who died after they were trapped in a cave; their story drew quite a bit of national press attention.

Despite the scope of that flood, the number of deaths was small when compared with some other disasters. In 1989, the Loma Prieta earthquake took 62 lives. The 1981 collapse of a skywalk, during a crowded dance at Kansas City's Hyatt Regency Hotel, killed 114 people. The 1988 bombing of Pan Am Flight 103, over Lockerbie, Scotland, resulted in 258 deaths. A 1943 fire at Boston's Coconut Grove nightclub took 493 lives.

If compared to the estimated 10,000 (or more) people who died as a result of an earthquake in India during 1993, our recent disasters may not seem very tragic at all. We are lucky we have not had more serious losses of lives in our country's recent disasters. But we never know when or where the next major disaster will strike here in the U.S., or how many lives it will take.

Sometimes the best way to gauge a disaster is just to listen to the stories of the survivors. Barr (1993) wrote this of the Great Mississippi/Midwest flood—"Liken it to a rude guest who crashes a party for 43 days [the length of time the Mississippi was above flood stage in the Quad Cities area], then steals away and leaves a terrific mess to clean up" (p. 1A). She goes on to offer these observations from another town resident:

> It's not over for us, not for a long ways. We still have stinking mud, up past your knees in some places. Now that it's down, it's almost worse. I can see accumulations of a lifetime that are gone. I don't have a thing that hasn't been touched by this flood in one way or another. (p. 1A)

Price (1993), also writing in the wake of the Great Flood, offers several other quotes that tell of both the emotional toll a major disaster takes on its victims and the strong fighting spirit that many will continue to show while in the face of adversity:

> Lots of folks already have said they'll never come back; guess I can't blame them.

> Well, at least it didn't get up to the second story. It got to the rooftops in Alexandria.

> I cooked everyone a Boots and Boats special [said one restaurant owner of the volunteers who sandbagged for her and saved her business]; if they came in boots and boats, they got free food.

> It's a horrible feeling to shovel sandbags until you're ready to drop only to watch that levee go; to watch it fill

your town and take away your homes . . . we all cried. We're still crying.

I'll never forget that night [of sandbagging] as long as I live [said a mayor]; I spent it holding my breath and praying a lot. If we had lost, it would have cost lives. But we won, and this community has a lot to be proud of. (p. 3A)

These are exactly the kinds of stories DMH workers will find themselves hearing, again and again.

Chapter 4

DEVELOPMENT AND EVOLUTION OF DISASTER MENTAL HEALTH STRATEGIES

There is evidence by Devine (1904) of early disaster relief efforts by social workers from the Chicago Relief and Aid Society, who assisted victims of the Chicago fire of 1871. Devine (1939) also documented how he administered the ARC operation that followed the San Francisco earthquake and fire of 1906. While the outpouring of goodwill may have been in some ways emotionally supportive and therapeutic, these early interventions focused primarily on meeting immediate needs for food, clothing, and shelter.

During World Wars I and II, mental health professionals were struggling to address the growing number of cases of *shell shock* (also known as *battle fatigue* and *combat stress*). A vast collection of symptoms and diagnoses often followed the stressful events that precipitated the condition, just as often happens with victims of major disasters. For many, getting them off the battlefield for some short period of rest and recuperation, and allowing them to "blow off steam," was enough to get them back in fighting form. These same issues, and the incidence of PTSD, have also been widely documented and studied among Vietnam vets (Freedman, Kaplan, & Sadock, 1972).

Probably the most widely known account of early crisis intervention that was truly DMH is the work of Lindemann (1944), which tells of acute grief reactions following the 1943 fire in Boston's Coconut Grove nightclub. Hundreds of the 493 people who perished in that fire were soldiers. Lindemann was working with the Psychiatry Department at Harvard Medical School and with the Massachusetts General Hospital at the time. He managed to help survivors and, simultaneously, document the various types of stress and discomfort they were experiencing.

Lindemann (1944) wrote about how similar the stories were, with victim after victim reporting shortness of breath, tightness in their throats, choking sensations, muscle weakness, and general feelings of emptiness, tension, and emotional pain. These symptoms would wax and wane, often worsening as events of the moment (e.g., someone visiting them to express sympathy) reminded them of their ordeal and current plight. He also found that recovery was faster and more thorough if victims were encouraged to express their grief and plan for the future.

Since then, people have detailed the DMH efforts that have followed most large disaster events. For example, Friedman and Linn (1957), two psychiatrists, were passengers on a cruise ship near Nantucket, Massachusetts, when survivors were brought aboard from the 1956 crash of two other luxury liners, the *Stockholm* and the *Andrea Doria*. They later reported their clinical observations:

> Survivors [initially] acted as if they had been sedated . . .
> people tended to act passively and compliantly. They
> displayed psychomotor retardation, flattening of affect,
> somnolence, and in some instances, amnesia for personal
> identification. They were nonchalant and easily suggest-
> ible. [Sometime later] they showed . . . an apparently
> compulsive need to tell the story again and again, with
> identical detail and emphasis. (p. 426)

This combination of stages of shock, suggestibility, and recovery has become known as the *disaster syndrome.*

Another well-documented disaster occurred in 1972. Considerable flooding took place in West Virginia when a Buffalo Creek mining company dam burst, killing 125 people and displacing 4,000 others. One group of researchers, Titchener, Kapp, and Winget (1976), found three levels of victim reaction.

The first level involved typical acute reactions to the event and related stressors, including insomnia, nightmares, memory difficulties, and anxiety with occasional panic episodes. The second level included symptoms and feelings of depression that persisted for months and, in some cases, for years. People had lost interest in social activities such as playing sports, hunting and fishing, and even in sexual relationships. Many had increased their smoking and alcohol consumption patterns. The third level revealed pervasive changes in attitude, lifestyle, and character. These victims had lower self-esteem, reported trouble trusting others, and had not successfully resolved their grief for those they lost. These most serious emotional casualties also were experiencing strong feelings of *survivor guilt.*

Lifton and Olson (1976), other Buffalo Creek researchers, also wrote about the so-called *survivor syndrome,* a name given to the array of short- and long-term symptoms that were noted in the preceding paragraphs. They listed five elements of the syndrome common among many victims:

1. Firmly established memories of the traumatic images of suffering from the event.
2. Guilt over having lived through it when others did not survive.
3. General feelings of numbing, sadness, and apathy, accompanied by social withdrawal.
4. Relationship difficulties as people struggle with competing feelings of suspicion of others while, at the same time, needing to become close to others.
5. A need to somehow bring closure to the event and find some personal meaning in all that has happened.

Explorations of disaster trauma that can be found in literature are not limited to the realms of physical and social sciences. Religious issues and pastoral counseling are also a part of most large relief operations. One example of this is offered by Jordan (1976), a minister who was working with the Buffalo Creek disaster victims and who detailed his ministerial and pastoral care experiences stemming from that assignment. He cautions members of the clergy to use the psychological tools that are available to them but to remember that their primary calling is as a pastor rather than a psychotherapist. He states, "faith resources offer hope and liberation that go beyond 'adjustment' and 'recovery'" (p. 170).

Heffron (1977) analyzed DMH efforts following the 1972 floods caused in Pennsylvania by Hurricane Agnes. Although only seven people were killed, over 20,000 people were left homeless, and property damage exceeded $1 billion, in what was then our nation's greatest disaster. His findings called for DMH workers to help victims focus on prevention of greater, long-term problems by focusing upon and resolving issues as they arose. He wrote of the positive effects of ventilating as a way to relieve stress, but emphasized that this must be done in such a way as to not leave victims feeling they have become mentally ill. Heffron also stressed the need for extensive use of outreach approaches and for helpers to watch out for their own, and each other's needs.

Literature on stress and coping is an important component of DMH. Seyle (1956) noted that almost any situation that changes the status quo, either positively *(eustress)* or negatively *(distress)*, will be stressful to those who must adapt to the changes. Seyle also introduced the concept known as the *general adaptation syndrome* (GAS), a form of stress-induced biological decompensation. More detail about GAS will be offered later in this book.

Janis (1958) and others have found that people can be *inoculated* against some of the negative stress reactions that are so often linked to pending stressful events. He provided preventive educational information to people who were going to have surgery and found that their emotional reactions were less serious than those of persons who had not received the same advance preparation. Meichenbaum (1985) and others using cognitive-behavioral therapy have since expanded the use of *stress-inoculation therapy.*

Holmes and Rahe (1967) present one example of how to weigh the relative values of various stressors. Death of a spouse is the stressor that is rated the highest on the list of events they studied. Their index allows a framework for determining scores based upon the total number of life change units (stress points) a person is attempting to handle at any moment in time. Their findings also suggest the likelihood that a person will become physically or mentally ill given certain higher level scores and the possibility of inadequate means of coping.

Seligman (1975) found that people can easily become overwhelmed by the loss of control over many aspects of their lives, which they experience following traumatic events. Some will stop routine functioning and fall prey to depression and what he dubbed *learned helplessness,* an often crippling state of physical and/or emotional inadequacy characterized by extreme dependence upon others. DMH efforts often need to help empower victims in order to return them to their former levels of confidence and competence.

Lindy and Grace (1985) and Bolin (1985) discuss the social support networks that develop following a disaster and the important role they can play during the recovery period. Lindy and Grace also note that, although one might guess that emotionally wounded victims would be quite wary of strangers and be overly protective of one another, DMH workers (and others in relief roles) can generally gain very easy access to victims — even to those individuals who appear to be suffering the most pain.

Their theory about this ready access centers on something these authors metaphorically dubbed a *trauma membrane* — basically a psychological security blanket that forms around the survivors in order to protect them from greater harm. It becomes the victims' choice (although often guided by friends and family) whether to let helpers permeate the membrane — whether to trust and confide in those they meet along their personal road to recovery. Although members of the media, tourists, and researchers may be shut out, helpers are generally granted entry to this private realm.

Mitchell (1983) wanted to help emergency responders cope with the distressing day-to-day events *(critical incidents)* they faced on the job. He recognized two main problem areas:

1. The initial impact of a traumatic emergency scene.
2. The ongoing stress reactions that occur during each person's recovery.

Drawing together information on combat stress, police psychology, the management of emotional trauma in emergency medical settings, and DMH, he formed a process he dubbed *Critical Incident Stress Debriefing* (CISD).

Critical incidents might be any events that deeply impact a team of helpers such as police, fire/rescue personnel, emergency room staffers, or ARC volunteers. Examples of such incidents might be witnessing a police officer or fire/rescue person being seriously injured or killed (or a police officer needing to take someone else's life) while on duty, being involved in an accident in which a rescue vehicle hits and harms or kills others, or helping clear an accident scene at which there had been several children hurt or killed. Almost any case that involves unusual circumstances, lots of media attention, or graphic memories might warrant a debriefing.

CISD teams had sprung up in many areas of the U.S. and in several other countries by the time Mitchell (1988) wrote a progress report on the spread of CISD for the same journal in which he had originally introduced the concepts. The Army, Air Force, and Navy have all developed DMH components that rely heavily upon CISD principles. The Navy's Special Psychiatric Rapid Intervention Teams (SPRINT) are one example. Military teams have helped out in situations such as Hurricane Andrew's devastation of Homestead Air Force Base in Florida and Typhoon Omar's assault on our soldiers based on Guam.

Mitchell and others have further refined the CISD process and have written extensively on issues relating to team building and training. One example is Clark and Friedman's (1992) article which cautions that debriefings clearly carry with them certain emotional risks and that "more damage than good may [result from debriefings] done by inexperienced, untrained individuals who lack a solid knowledge base" (p. 32). More detail about the CISD process is provided later in this book.

Carson and Butcher (1992) discuss coping strategies as falling into one of two general categories, *task-oriented* or *defense-oriented* responses. Persons using a task-oriented approach will be actively using problem-solving techniques to resolve their stressors. They appraise the situation, select a course of action, and actively pursue a positive outcome. Defense-oriented persons will, instead, assume a protective posture. They more often engage in excessive crying, use of negative defense mechanisms (denial and repression), and social isolation. Their recovery will tend to take longer and be less successful.

Federal government involvement in disaster relief began with passage of the Disaster Act of 1950. Year after year, as more disasters occurred, revisions to that original piece of legislation continued to result in needed improvements to the federal response system (Siporin, 1987). NIMH (now CMHS) was established as part of the National Mental Health Act of 1946 for the broad purposes of combating mental illness and promoting mental health through various research and training initiatives. In 1972, NIMH's Center for Studies of Suicide Prevention evolved into the Mental Health Emergencies Section, and its mission increasingly became more interested in crisis intervention programs of all sorts (Resnik, H.L. Ruben, & D.D. Ruben, 1975).

In the wake of serious floods in Rapid City, South Dakota, and Wilkes-Barre, Pennsylvania, Congress held hearings and then passed an even more comprehensive piece of legislation — the Disaster Relief Act of 1974 (Parad et al., 1975a). That bill mandated NIMH to provide services to victims of natural disasters and training to relief workers. NIMH has taken a leading role in the DMH field since that time.

NIMH has also been involved in DMH with catastrophes other than natural disasters. One example is Frederick's (1981) examination of the results of the 1977 conference on aircraft accidents that NIMH cosponsored, which compares and contrasts the needs of air crash survivors with those who are victims of weather-related events.

Many older CMHS (NIMH) pamphlets and books concerning disaster relief are referenced throughout this book. Also referenced is an excellent new work, *Disaster Response and Recovery: A Handbook for Mental Health Professionals* (Myers, 1994), which I was fortunate enough to be allowed to preview during the preparation of this manuscript. Readers who are interested in learning more about DMH are urged to obtain a copy of it.

Tierney and Baisden (1979) point out another key organization in the history of disaster research: Ohio State University's Disaster Research Center. Formed in 1963, the center focuses upon the social aspects of disaster. The Center has teams of trained researchers ready to go whenever disaster research opportunities occur. They have published hundreds of studies that examine the various ways in which organizations and communities respond to traumatic events.

Readers interested in a broader overview of DMH are referred to Ahearn and Cohen (1984) for a more thorough review. They present an annotated bibliography of 297 works covering subcategories including theory of disaster behavior; physical and mental health effects upon individuals, families, groups, and communities; coping and recovery; mental health and relief services for victims; and prevention.

Solomon and Green (1992) have conducted an even more recent survey of the literature, focusing on the long-term mental health effects of exposure to disaster situations. Their conclusion is that for natural disasters, "psychological consequences may persist as long as three years, though most symptoms seem to abate by about 16 months . . . [while the] consequences of human-caused disasters may persist even longer" (p. 1). They go on to caution that recovery statistics are based upon group averages, which "tend to disguise the fact that while many individuals may recover quickly from their disaster experiences, others may take much longer to recover, if indeed they recover at all" (p. 1).

Recent literature covers various aspects of just about every natural and human caused disaster event that has occurred. The one rather glaring exception, however, is that research does not yet seem to be available to directly support the efficacy of most DMH interventions. With that exception, be assured that you can easily find more to read on DMH.

Chapter 5

THE PSYCHOLOGICAL AFTERMATH OF A DISASTER

During a recent seminar on DMH, Garrison, E. Reese, and M. Reese (1993) spoke of their experiences with victims seen following various disasters, especially Hurricane Andrew. Garrison highlighted some of the typical features and memories displayed or described by the survivors, such as their blank stares, reported numbing of emotions, and disorientation. People tended to mark time differently, simply talking about events as being before the storm or after it. The sounds of the wind and the rain (and other, similar markers) were firmly etched in their memories.

Garrison went on to speak about the moments immediately following the disaster, when survivors were probably beginning to search their brains' memory banks for any similar events that they might be able to draw upon for guidance and strength. Unfortunately, most people probably found nothing comparable which could help them. Faced with a major trauma, most people simply cannot carry on with business as usual.

To illustrate his point, Garrison told a story about a police officer, himself a victim, who was asked by his supervisor to go out following Andrew and watch traffic on a busy local highway. Hours later, the supervisor found the officer in the middle of a major traffic jam because he was just watching traffic, as he had been told, rather than directing it as the supervisor had actually wanted him to do. The officer was still traumatized and was probably trying to regain composure and assess his own losses. He was not yet in any shape to be of much help to others.

Several formulations can be offered to illustrate what goes on in victims' minds as they anticipate, experience, and strive to recover from disasters. The first to be explored is a biological model. Seyle's (1956) general adaptation syndrome outlines three specific phases of human biological response to stressors: *alarm, resistance,* and *exhaustion.*

Alarm can begin either at the point at which someone begins to anticipate a pending stressor or after something actually occurs. The autonomic nervous system activates the involuntary responses associated with what Cannon (1929) dubbed our *fight or flight* mechanism. Blood pressure rises, respiratory and heart rates increase, blood clotting propensity is enhanced, and so on, as we enter a more heightened state of arousal. No matter whether the threat is physical or emotional, the physiological reactions remain the same as the body mobilizes for defensive and/or offensive action.

The *resistance phase* occurs while our bodies continue to carry out their primary mission—trying to do whatever is necessary to cope with the stressors and return things to a more normal state. In disasters, this is synonymous with the period of cleanup, rebuilding, and recovery activities.

Exhaustion results when the stress levels remain too high for too long a period. Victims and helpers who have not rested, and have not properly managed their stress, find themselves becoming ill, physically and/or mentally, as they succumb to the pressures they are under. Those who recognize the warning signs and take appropriate remedial action will likely have more positive outcomes. Those who miss (or ignore) the signs, or who develop defense-oriented postures (and do not problem-solve), typically will have more negative overall outcomes.

This biological formulation can be applied to any type of major stress. Those that follow are more specifically geared for the situations that DMH workers will be facing.

Kafrissen, Heffron, and Zusman (1975) list and define seven stages of time through which the victims and communities hit by a disaster will progress:

- *Alarm* (or warning phase)—present in disasters with slow, more predictable onset and a time when stress levels are rising.
- *Threat*—period of imminent danger and assessment of degree to which real threat exists.

- *Impact*—time during which the event occurs, normally a time of tension but not panic.
- *Inventory*—people get out and survey the damage and, while it may seem to be a highly stressful period of mass confusion, recovery begins.
- *Rescue*—some will show evidence of the disaster syndrome, as efforts to assist the victims are undertaken.
- *Remedy*—morale is high for many, but the stress is taking its toll on others during what is possibly the longest phase, and the time when large-scale relief efforts take place.
- *Restoration* (or recovery)—this point is the "light at the end of the tunnel," and the point for which everyone has been waiting. (pp. 160-161)

Farberow and Gordon (1981) write that these stages are more useful for sociological studies than DMH work. Far more valuable for mental health workers, they believe, is the formulation of four emotional phases that most disaster victims experience during the recovery process:

- *Heroic phase*
- *Honeymoon phase*
- *Disillusionment phase*
- *Reconstruction phase* (pp. 3-4)

The *heroic phase* begins immediately, as people work together to do whatever they can to prevent loss of life and property. Anyone who watched television coverage of the thousands of volunteers filling and placing sandbags along the Mississippi River and its tributaries during the 1993 floods, or the more recent California floods of 1995, has witnessed the excitement and the intensity of effort that exists in this phase.

The *honeymoon phase* is next. This will be a period of 2 weeks to 2 months during which the victims' spirits have been lifted by events such as the outpouring of relief supplies; support from friends, family, and even total strangers; and promises of additional aid from community agencies and the various levels of government. Optimism runs high, but will be short-lived.

The *disillusionment phase* follows, all too quickly, and lasts anywhere from several months to a year (or more). Bureaucracy enters the equation and everything seems to take far too long. Promised aid does not materialize or falls short of expectations. Victims tend to give up their wait for help from others and begin to get on with their lives, somehow solving their own problems. Again television images may come to mind, if you recall seeing film crews revisit major disaster sites on the anniversary of the event. For instance, many southern Florida residents were still homeless on the first anniversary of Hurricane Andrew. Too many of them were still victims—victims of zoning law changes, FEMA regulations, bankrupt insurance companies, and crooked builders.

The *reconstruction phase* is the period during which individuals and communities work to reestablish normal (predisaster) functioning. It can easily last several years.

TYPICAL REACTIONS AND NEEDS OF VICTIMS

CMHS's *Training Manual for Human Service Workers in Major Disasters* (Farberow, 1978d) offers this summary of the most common needs, reactions, and feelings experienced by persons who have been directly or indirectly exposed to a disaster:

1. Basic survival concerns.
2. Grief over loss of loved ones and/or prized possessions.
3. Separation anxiety and fears for safety of significant others.
4. Regressive behavior (e.g., thumb sucking in children).
5. Relocation and isolation anxieties.
6. Need to express thoughts and feelings about having experienced the disaster.
7. Need to feel one is part of the community and its rebuilding efforts.
8. Altruism and the desire to help others cope and rebuild their lives. (p. 26)

What relief workers will specifically encounter will depend upon the point in time at which they arrive for their assignment. First-responders, coming on the scene within the first few days, will obviously get a different picture of the victims than will someone who arrives weeks later, at a different stage of recovery.

Local health, safety, and relief workers are subject to the same mix of reactions and emotions that is being discussed throughout this section. They may become temporarily incapacitated, as was the case with the police officer who was watching rather than directing traffic. This is one very good reason for calling in outside help, be it ARC workers, soldiers from our military and National Guard, or representatives of the many other relief organizations. The hope is that the people brought into the disaster zone from elsewhere will arrive fresh, they will be ready to roll up their sleeves and go to work, and they will be far less prone to being preoccupied with personal and family issues of recovery.

Everyone working the disaster is subjected to long hours and stressful working conditions. The helpers who are brought into an area must adjust to the new environment and its potentially dangerous features. There might be aftershocks, additional flooding, insects, snakes, or other unusual challenges to confront. These features of the assignment can quickly fatigue the responders.

The following sections provide more detailed descriptions of the ways persons from different age groups respond to disasters. Other special target populations will also be discussed.

REACTIONS OF
CHILDREN AND ADOLESCENTS

Disasters often cause behavioral changes and regression in children. Many react with fear and show clear signs of anxiety about recurrence of the disaster event(s). Sleep disturbances are very common among children (and adults) and can best be handled by quickly returning to (or establishing) a familiar bedtime routine. Inability to do this proved to be a major problem following the Los Angeles earthquake, as frequent aftershocks and displaced residences made it difficult for anyone to return to regular sleep routines. Many families were all sleeping together in the same bed long after the main quake.

Similarly, school avoidance may occur and can lead to development of school phobias if children are not quickly returned to their normal routine of school attendance. In some disasters, the schools, themselves, may be flooded (or damaged in another way), making them inoperable. This, and the need to be bused to other, unfamiliar buildings, will further add to the stresses on the children. The Los Angeles earthquake and its aftershocks resulted in many children staying home for weeks, fearful to leave their parents' sides for the length of a school day.

Farberow and Gordon (1981, pp. 11-15) and Lystad (1985, pp. 63-66) list several other typical, age-related reactions of young people:

Preschool Children

crying	irritability	confusion
clinging	eating problems	immobility
sadness	speech problems	baby talk

sensitivity to loud noises
fears of animals, darkness, and/or the weather
nightmares/night terrors
needing people nearby and/or lights on in order to sleep
wanting help with feeding/getting dressed/and so on
loss of bowel/bladder control
fear of being left alone and/or fear of strangers

Latency Age Children (6-11 Years Old)

This age group may show many of the preceding symptoms, plus:

irrational fears	headaches	nausea
visual problems	hearing problems	disobedience
distractibility	trouble concentrating	fighting
peer problems	social withdrawal	

school refusal and/or behavioral problems in school
inability to enjoy previously pleasurable activities

Preadolescence and
Adolescence (12-17 Years Old)

headaches (or other physical complaints)
depression, possibly with suicidal ideation
confusion
poor performance
aggressive behavior
withdrawal and social isolation
sleep disturbances (including excessive sleep)
school problems (academic and behavioral)
antisocial behavior (stealing and vandalism)

Timing of onset of these changes varies with each person, as does duration. Some symptoms occur immediately, while others may not show until weeks later. Just about all of these things are considered normal reactions, as long as they do not last for more than several weeks.

ADULT REACTIONS

Farberow (1978a, 1978d) also provides more detail about typical adult responses. Adults often report mild symptoms of depression and anxiety. They can feel haunted by visual memories of the event. They may experience psychosomatic illnesses. Preexisting physical problems such as heart trouble, diabetes, and ulcers may worsen in response to the increased level of stress. They may show anger, mood swings, suspicion, irritability, and apathy. Changes in appetite and sleep patterns are quite common. Adults, too, may have a period of poor performance at work or school and may undergo some social withdrawal.

Middle-aged adults, in particular, may experience additional stress if they lose the security of their planned (and possibly paid-off) retirement home (or their financial nest egg), and if they are forced to pay for extensive rebuilding costs. Older adults will greatly miss their daily routines and will suffer strong feelings of loss from missing friends and loved ones. They may also suffer feelings of significant loss from the absence of their home or apartment or its sentimental objects (especially items like paintings, antiques, family Bibles, photo albums, and films or videotapes) which tied them to their past.

Readers will quickly begin to notice that there is considerable overlap between some of the common feelings and behavioral symptoms noted previously and the following list of warning signs of mental illness. Recent estimates are that one person in every six or seven (15% of the population) has a diagnosable form of mental illness at any given time. This is true across all age groups, races, economic and ethnic groups, and for both sexes (Weaver, 1993b).

Prolonged exposure to stress may also bring out previously undiagnosed illness in persons who have never shown any signs of mental illness. When individuals already diagnosed as being mentally ill are faced with the added burden of disaster-related stress, those persons may experience an exacerbation of symptoms.

Here is a review of several of the most common warning signs of mental illness:

1. Prolonged feelings of anxiety and/or despair
2. Inability to concentrate and/or to make decisions
3. Changes in habits (e.g., eating, sleeping, or sexual activity)
4. Changes in personality (e.g., a quiet, shy, cautious person begins to live dangerously)
5. Loss of self-esteem (e.g., feelings of extreme guilt after an arrest or the loss of one's job)
6. Withdrawal from others/social isolation
7. Symptoms of disordered thought processes:
   a. Undue suspiciousness of others
   b. Belief people are talking about, laughing at, or trying to somehow control him/her
   c. Hears voices and/or sees things
   d. Believes television, radio, and/or print media are addressing him/her
   e. E.S.P. or telepathy
   f. Grandiosity
   g. Religious preoccupation
8. Misdirected anger/desire for revenge
9. Extreme dependency

10. Exaggerated fears
11. Physical problems without any organic cause
12. Mood swings
13. Performance is not up to par
14. Compulsions/rituals (e.g., too frequent hand washing)
15. Thoughts of harming self or others (includes overt statements/acts as well as covert moves, e.g., getting one's affairs in order as though preparing for death). (pp. 9-10)

Everyone may experience some of these symptoms from time to time, and it is often quite normal to do so, especially in the period following a major stressful event like a disaster. But when several of these symptoms are experienced at once, they persist for long periods of time, and they are interfering with daily functioning, or when any of the higher risk symptoms (e.g., suicidal thoughts) are experienced, more help than a short-term DMH intervention is probably needed.

Community disruption, changes in routine, loss of social supports, rumors, misinformation, and bad weather can all have a profoundly negative impact upon adults' ability to cope and to carry on with the tasks of recovery. Moreover, adding to all of the other pressures they are facing, adults have the responsibility of caring for children and adolescents who are looking to them for the structure, strength, and guidance that they need in order to carry on during these stressful times. All of this added stress can result in increased potential for substance abuse, marital/relationship conflicts, domestic violence, and child abuse.

Adults living in group residential rehabilitation settings (mental health, mental retardation, or drug and alcohol facilities) and institutions (prisons, hospitals, boarding homes, or nursing facilities) may react in the same ways others in the community react to the disaster. For these groups, there is often an overriding sense of isolation and dependence, which they may be made to feel even more strongly during the recovery period. Family members and friends are often lost, as actual casualties of the disaster itself or as captives of the cleanup effort. Either way, the persons in the residential settings generally receive less social contact and will tend to feel more forgotten and alone.

Parad et al. (1975b) profiled another group of victims whom DMH workers will sometimes encounter. He calls them *crisis prone* individuals. These are the clients who seem to more frequently and/or more seriously encounter problems in their everyday lives. He characterizes them this way:

Typically, the crisis prone person lacks or is unable to utilize the personal, family, and social supports that help everyone to cope with stress while functioning in everyday roles. Often alienated from meaningful and lasting interpersonal relations, he [or she] may exhibit some or all of the following interrelated problems:

1. Difficulty learning from experience.
2. A history of frequent crises, ineffectively resolved because of poor coping ability.
3. A history of mental disorder or other serious emotional disturbance.
4. Low self-esteem, which may be masked by provocative behavior.
5. A tendency toward impulsive "acting-out" behavior (doing without thinking).
6. Marginal income.
7. Lack of regular, fulfilling work.
8. Unsatisfying marriage and family relations.
9. Heavy drinking or other substance abuse.
10. History of numerous accidents.
11. Frequent encounters with law-enforcement agencies.
12. Frequent changes in address. (p. 26)

Obviously, survivors (and helpers) who fit this rather ominous characterization will be more challenging to work with than most of the people you will be seeing while on assignment.

ISSUES OF DIVERSITY

The victims' educational backgrounds and socioeconomic status may affect willingness to seek or accept assistance for their disaster-related psychological needs. Many people who have had less formal education and who have lower incomes tend to have negative attitudes about the value of DMH services. The key to reaching this population is to provide effective outreach services. Upper-income individuals, on the other hand, may see the value in DMH outreach services but decline help anyway, because the services are free and they do not want to take anything they perceive to be charity.

There can also be a wide range of racial, ethnic, and cultural variety represented in a disaster area, and this generally leads to a broad spectrum of psychological responses. Sometimes even a seemingly homogeneous community will contain pockets of persons from an entirely different culture, which relief workers never expected to find there.

For instance, a Midwestern farming community may temporarily be home to a large group of Latino migrant workers who were traveling with the harvest season and happened to get caught in a flood zone. A language barrier is just one of many possible complications that may impede the delivery of services to that group of victims. Assigning relief workers who are familiar with the target population would be the ideal situation, but it is not always possible. All workers need to be sensitive to the special customs, beliefs, and needs of the various groups they serve.

Chapter 6

KEY DISASTER
MENTAL HEALTH CONCEPTS

Research suggests that people respond to disasters in fairly predictable ways. NIMH has published a variety of pamphlets and books that address the basic information needed by those who undertake a DMH assignment. These concepts are excerpted from several NIMH publications, including the *Training Manual for Human Service Workers in Major Disasters* (Farberow, 1978d), the *Field Manual for Human Service Workers in Major Disasters* (Farberow, 1978a), and the *Manual for Child Health Workers in Major Disasters* (Farberow & Gordon, 1981), as well as from personal experiences.

1. **The Target Population Is Primarily Normal.** Many DMH workers come from primary work settings in which they diagnose and treat clients with various forms of mental illness. In a disaster setting, the vast majority of individuals you will encounter are just everyday people who functioned well prior to the crisis and are capable of doing so again, given a bit of temporary assistance, guidance, and support.

2. **Mental Health Labels Should Be Avoided.** When workers expect healthy responses (rather than pathological ones), they are more likely to get them. Also, victims (or disaster relief staff and volunteers) who sense they are being viewed as crazy or weak are highly prone to rejecting services from DMH workers, simply as a matter of pride.

   Myers (1985) suggests DMH workers characterize themselves via the use of terms like crisis counselor or crisis worker. It is usually better to portray yourself as a crisis intervention or stress management specialist, because those roles tend to be far less threatening to persons who become uncomfortable around anyone they believe to be mental health professionals (psychiatrists, psychologists, psychiatric social workers, counselors, therapists, or psychiatric nurses).

3. **People Do Not Disintegrate.** Although some transitory disturbance in functioning is to be expected in persons who have been subjected to severe stress, most will continue to carry on with their lives in a manner which will often be so goal-directed and effective that it will surprise first-time disaster workers. As victims do work to rebuild their lives, natural emotions such as frustration, helplessness, and anger may appear and will need to be recognized and channeled.

4. **Victims (and Relief Workers) Respond to DMH Workers Who Show Active Interest and Concern.** Although a disaster may hit hundreds (or thousands) of people in any given area, the effect it has upon many of the individual victims (and helpers) is to leave them feeling isolated and alone. Getting people talking, just by being a good listener, is a good way to start breaking through that pain and reconnecting people with the world around them. Victims like to tell their stories, and it takes relatively little work to get helpful conversations started.

5. **Workers Need to Abandon Traditional Office-Based Approaches.** Workers need to be proactive. Rather than waiting for intervention opportunities to arise, DMH staff should be actively seeking chances to intervene. Venturing out to the site of the disaster works wonders for people who are out there cleaning up and getting on with their lives. It can also be enough of a gesture of support that it can help get some victims who have not gone back to their homes to take that important first step.

Home visits are just a small part of the outreach that is sure to be needed. DMH workers may also have to spend some time visiting hospitals, schools, community centers, and other gathering places in order to best serve victims who will not necessarily come into a center to seek services or emotional support.

6. **Be Sensitive to Cultural, Ethic, Racial, and Socioeconomic Diversity.** DMH work often requires workers to travel far from their homes and to practice their skills in places that are quite different from their usual surroundings. FEMA (1981) reported that the five obstacles to effective worker and victim communication were:

- Language
- Nonverbal communication
- Preconceptions and stereotypes
- The tendency to judge others
- High anxiety

Consequently, it is imperative that workers become attuned to the specific needs of the people and communities in which they will be serving. Workers must take special care to be sure to treat everyone with respect and allow others to maintain their dignity.

7. **The Disaster Climate Tends to Generate Many Rumors.** People in the communities that have been struck by the event (and their friends and relatives across the country) will desperately crave accurate and timely information about the damage and the recovery efforts. Regular channels of communication, like the telephone system, may be out of commission. Helpers need to do their best to provide simple, factual information about all aspects of the disaster and the ensuing relief programs, including DMH.

8. **Disasters Bring Out the Best and the Worst In People.** Be prepared to see people at their best—pitching in, working together, and helping others in their times of greatest need. Volunteers and donations (money and needed supplies) generally pour into the affected area, and you will feel extremely proud to be a part of it all. But be aware that you may also encounter evidence of people at their worst. Some people see disasters as an opportunity to loot, ripoff, price gouge, cheat, and swindle the already downtrodden and unsuspecting residents of the area (and bilk the organizations that come to their aid). This kind of blatant victimization

can greatly lower the morale of both the survivors and the helpers.

9. **Helpers Are Subject to a Vast Array of Physical and Emotional Responses to Crises, Including Burnout.** My own DMH work has led me to experience some of the most exhilarating feelings of my professional career; every chance I get, I tell others about it and try to recruit more workers. Still, I must caution others that this kind of work is not for everyone.

   Before jumping into an assignment, people may well need to acquire some additional training, especially if they plan to enter the ARC DSHR system. What is more important, they must seriously assess their own motivation, strengths, needs, weaknesses, obligations, and support system in order to determine whether they are up to the many challenges that lie ahead.

10. **Workers Can Find Strength (and Peer Supports) in Numbers.** Nothing short of a hostage situation can take a group of perfect strangers, place them in a common predicament, and gel them into a state of absolute camaraderie faster than a disaster assignment. Within 48 hours of arrival, relationships have developed that an outside observer might perceive as lifelong friendships. This sense of closeness becomes a key factor in stress management for those who respond to calls for help and head for disaster relief settings.

11. **One DMH Experience Is Enough to Get You Hooked.** Be forewarned that, for many of us, DMH work has proven to be highly addictive. Once you get a taste of it, you too may want to go out on assignments as often as your schedule will allow. In fact, it may even change the way you perceive the world. Whenever I see news coverage or weather reports about disaster-related phenomena, I find myself wishing I could be there helping out. Once I retire (or hit the lottery), I am planning to devote more time to my own ARC disaster volunteer career.

   Of course I do need to do a bit more work with my wife on this vision of our retirement. Right now our children are still young, and she is not ready to look that far ahead. I hope to one day get her hooked too. She knows how much this means to me and, as this little story will illustrate, she is being very understanding about it.

I was out on my first job in March, 1993. When I returned and told her how much I enjoyed it, she said it was okay with her if I went off and did this once a year. When the Mississippi River/Midwest flooding began a short 2 months later, ARC asked for me again. I mentioned it to her but she reminded me we had agreed to my going out only once per year. I turned ARC down.

As the days and weeks rolled by, we watched the situation in the Midwest deteriorate on the evening news; the flooding was becoming worse and worse. I had not said anything more to her about it, but one evening after the news, she turned to me and said, "You better go." That was all I needed to hear. I went out with her blessing.

Chapter 7

THE CONTEXT
OF RESPONSE

The task of bringing order to the chaos wrought by a disaster is shared by many local, state, and federal governmental officials and agencies (including the military); thousands of ARC volunteers and staff; members of the Salvation Army; representatives of numerous religiously affiliated relief organizations; claims adjusters from insurance companies; people who support various service organizations; and countless other public and private agencies and individuals. The next few sections will explore some of the mechanics of a disaster response.

PLANNING FOR DISASTERS

The job of cleaning up and returning things to normal following a disaster actually begins long before it even occurs, with many, many disaster preparedness meetings and constant writing, practice sessions, and revision of disaster action plans. FEMA, together with state level emergency management agencies (EMA) and other local, state, and federal governmental bodies, must have plans in place and ready to execute for foreseeable emergencies. EMAs that often grew out of the old Civil Defense units — those same people who sounded sirens and got us to take cover under our desks at school or in fallout shelters during the Cold War — now help communities with many other types of disaster planning and response.

In your own area there are, no doubt, plans in place for events such as large fires, weather emergencies, hazardous material spills, transportation accidents (e.g., airplane or train crashes), and so on. Depending upon where you live, there may also be plans for nuclear plant-related evacuation, terrorist activity, or other, more unusual occurrences.

Apart from the obvious plans made by government officials and the local ARC chapter, there should be plans in place in hospitals, schools, residential facilities (and in most large buildings of any kind), airports, and so on. You might be surprised at some of the detailed plans that have been written by large corporations.

Sometimes disaster plans are kept very current; they are well written and detailed, aspects of them are regularly rehearsed, and they are well publicized. Other times they are old, too brief, infrequently circulated, or for some similar reason of little worth. Many of the relatively good plans are still weak in the areas of mental health needs and preparedness.

One of the ways a DMH worker can help out at the planning stage of the process is to request and review copies of the disaster plans covering his or her community. Although the mental health aspects of disasters have been broadly documented and publicized for many years, few plans make satisfactory provision for the significant level of DMH involvement that is needed when disasters strike.

GETTING STARTED IN
DISASTER MENTAL HEALTH

There are a variety of ways to become involved in DMH work. Those who are employed in community mental health settings, hospitals (especially emergency rooms or trauma centers), crisis intervention units, or human service agencies of any kind are potential candidates for relief work in a disaster. When something is happening nearby, your employer may be asked to lend some staff to help out.

The story of my own start in DMH will illustrate how sometimes a twist of fate can bring about this change in one's career direction. I have been in the mental health field for 20 years, and I have done a great deal of emergency mental health work, including hotline telephone counseling, home visits, screening people for (and arranging) voluntary hospital admissions, as well as doing involuntary commitments. As often happens with many veteran workers who have spent their full-time employment careers in the public sector, I can seem rather hardened and cynical at times. After all, in my day we were taught not to allow professional experiences to affect us emotionally and not to take work home with us; I tended to be quite good at both of these things.

Despite so many years of interest and work in crisis intervention, it was by virtue of an accidental occurrence that I began doing DMH. About 3 years ago a light plane crashed in the driveway of a home in my area. The pilot, an 18-year-old who had just gotten his license the day before, was circling a community pool, waving to friends. Something caused the plane to tip and it headed straight into the ground.

There, a teenage woman was moving her car from one side of the driveway to the other. She was about to go off to college and needed an oil change before the trip. Her younger brother was standing nearby waiting to do the job for her. Her stepmother was nearby, too. The plane landed squarely over the driver's seat of her car. Both car and plane immediately burst into flames, probably killing the pilot and the young woman instantaneously, as the brother and stepmother watched in horror.

I got a call from someone on the ambulance crew that responded to the scene; the girl's father was an active member of their fire/rescue squad, and they wanted some crisis intervention staff members to come out and help him and his family cope with the tragedy. I took three other staff members with me and we spent several hours there, doing whatever we could to provide support. They continued to have contact with me occasionally, over a period of about 16 months. As time passed, I watched them progress through several stages of recovery. I formed such a strong link with them that my eyes are tearing up even as I write this brief summary of the event.

Two of the three staff members who went with me that day told me afterwards that they never wanted to do that sort of thing again—it was too emotionally stressful for them. For some reason I reacted differently. Perhaps it was because I had some familiarity with the literature on DMH. Whatever the reason, that one case got me hooked.

Other new DMH friends have told me similar stories. One fellow, for instance, came upon the scene of a bus crash, helped out, and later realized his interest had been kindled. Another local social worker first became curious about DMH when she spoke to a man who worked as a team member for a large airline's crash response team. Her husband knew of her interest and, when he saw press coverage of my DMH activities, he suggested she give it a try. She did, and now she is hooked. She and I have since met and now we work together on local ARC projects.

If you are new and you do not want to wait for your special calling to DMH, consider volunteering with your local ARC Chapter, CISD team, or fire/rescue squad. Working with one or more of these groups can be a good way to "get your feet wet." You will be able to meet and work with others doing similar work and you will begin to develop a sense about whether this is something you may enjoy, have the time to do, and can physically and emotionally tolerate.

AMERICAN RED CROSS (ARC)
AND THE DISASTER SERVICES
HUMAN RESOURCES (DSHR) SYSTEM

As *The Disaster Services Human Resources System Member's Handbook* (ARC, 1987) proudly points out, ARC has been serving people in disaster situations since 1881 when, in the state of Michigan, residents experienced destructive forest fires. Since then, ARC has grown in size to about 3,000 chapters throughout the country. ARC has also taken on a formal mandate to carry out disaster-related responsibilities. In 1905, the organization received a congressional charter "to undertake relief activities for the purpose of mitigating the suffering caused by disaster" (p. 7).

ARC is an independent, nonprofit organization, funded by the generous gifts of the American people. ARC works very hard at being a good steward of these donated funds. The recipients are made aware that ARC assistance is indeed a gift.

Preparedness is the key element in ARC's ability to carry out its mandate. Through detailed planning and cooperative relationships with many levels of government (and numerous other private and public agencies, corporations, and individuals), the staff and thousands of volunteer DSHR members have been trained and are ready for deployment.

ARC pays for all travel, lodging, and meal expenses for its workers (staff members and volunteers) on assignment. Disaster travelers usually receive an advance check before leaving home, so that they can pay for meals, ground transportation, laundry, and so on. Airfare and room costs are centrally billed to ARC whenever it is possible to do so. Careful documentation of expenses is required, and training in how to properly complete the necessary paperwork is offered as part of each person's initial orientation.

Volunteers are generally asked to make a 3-week commitment prior to being sent out. Sometimes shorter amounts of time are okay. DMH workers tend to have trouble getting away from their employment or private practices for long periods of time. Because DMH specialists are so greatly needed, and yet are still in relatively short supply, 10-day commitments are often acceptable.

ARC volunteers serving at disasters here in the United States come from all over the country and, sometimes, from other countries, especially Canada and Mexico. They represent all ages, races, cultures, and socioeconomic backgrounds. Thus, there is quite a bit of diversity represented in any given job. Many couples have found ways to travel and work together on ARC assignments. There are also many retired persons. Working with ARC is a great way to meet lots of nice people.

ARC takes extra care to avoid any situations that would reflect unfavorably upon the organization. Volunteers and staff members are carefully screened and trained for their relief roles. Workers are also told not to wear ARC clothing or logo items when off the job, in order to help safeguard the organization's public image.

ARC DISASTER SERVICES

Blood banking services, mass care feeding, and sheltering victims are probably the most widely known emergency services provided by ARC during small- or large-scale disasters. Far more help is available from ARC when verified needs exist and other forms of aid are absent.

Help is made available in three stages: Phase one involves mass care (feeding and sheltering victims) and damage assessment. Phase two is the period when family services (casework) functions are performed to help people get back on their feet.

Phase three is essentially aftercare, a time when additional assistance is provided to anyone who seems to have fallen through the cracks in the whole relief system.

ARC can assist with purchases of replacement clothing, food, beds, and bedding; health care needs (e.g., lost prescription medications, glasses, dentures, and prosthetic devices); tools needed to carry on an occupation; and supplies for cleaning a residence (and doing minor repairs). ARC can also help with costs of rent and purchases of some necessary furnishings (e.g., refrigerators and stoves).

ARC carefully checks to be sure that other funding sources (e.g., insurance settlements and various types of governmental assistance) are explored first, so that ARC monies can always be available for those who fall through gaps in the other systems. Once victims' needs have been verified and properly documented, they receive ARC disbursing orders (DOs) for whatever items they have qualified to receive.

People can then go shopping with the DOs as though the DOs were cash, at whatever merchants the people have selected, and purchase brand-new replacement items. This process allows victims to start feeling a sense of renewed control over their lives. Simultaneously, this helps stimulate the local economy by putting money into businesses that generally were also negatively impacted by the disaster.

To do all that needs to be done, ARC has workers trained in four direct service specialties (mass care, health services, family service, and disaster welfare inquiry). There are many more people trained for several other internal and external support service specialties, including accounting, buildings and repair, communications, computer operations, damage assessment, fund raising, various liaison positions, logistics, public affairs, records and reports, staffing, supply, and training.

DMH began as part of health services and is the latest addition to ARC's array of services. Although staff and volunteers at all levels had always encouraged ventilation and provided emotional support to victims (and fellow helpers), it became increasingly obvious that more resources needed to be developed.

ARC DSHR TRAINING
AND CAREER OPTIONS

To get started as a DSHR volunteer, everyone needs to take a 3-hour "Introduction to Disaster" course, which is a concise, video-based training program. Everyone must also complete a 6-hour "Standard First Aid" course (3 hours of which is adult cardio pulmonary resuscitation [CPR]), a 6-hour "Serving the Diverse Community" course (dealing with consumer issues), and the training for their own specialty area. DMH workers get a 15-hour DMH course that introduces them to the basic concepts of the work they will be doing, and provides more details about practicing in an ARC relief effort.

DMH workers must be licensed (or similarly credentialed) professionals such as social workers, psychologists, psychiatrists, counselors, or nurses, and they must travel with a copy of their license (or credential). Others who might be interested in serving, but who do not have a license (or credential), can become family service workers or can become members of many of the other specializations. Those roles are equally important, many allow opportunities for directly helping victims, and ARC can always use more quality volunteers for every specialization.

Entry level DSHR staff and volunteers are called technicians (or techs). This is true despite any other titles or degrees a person may hold. As techs gain additional work experience, through being part of more and more disasters, they can move up to supervisory positions, first becoming specialists, then coordinators, assistant officers, and officers. To be promoted requires having had a certain number of assignments, getting good written evaluations, and obtaining quite a bit of cross-training in other ARC specialties. The ability to serve for longer periods of time on each assignment tends also to be helpful.

Those who are so inclined can change roles and go all the way to the top. They can become service center or shelter managers, district directors, assistant (or deputy) directors, or even operations directors. Every ARC position has a corresponding written job description that spells out the duties and responsibilities of the position and the types of training and experience that are required of candidates for the jobs.

GETTING A CALL AND GOING
ON ASSIGNMENT WITH ARC

When a disaster strikes (or is anticipated), the call to go out on the job will come through your local chapter. If you are not in an area served by a chapter, you may directly receive the DSHR contact from ARC headquarters. You are asked if you can accept the assignment, and you are given time to check with family members and employers. ARC understands that volunteers cannot always drop everything and go whenever they are asked to do so.

Those times when you do agree to go, you will be given information about making travel arrangements, what to pack, where you are to report upon arrival, and what the anticipated conditions there will be. Sometimes you may be waiting for several days to see how an event unfolds and what staffing needs develop; other times you may be asked to fly immediately (or the next day).

Upon arrival, all ARC workers check in at the disaster headquarters office. There is paperwork to complete and your blood pressure and overall health status will be checked. People can be sent home if their health status (e.g., high blood pressure) might put them at risk were they to stay on the job. Next, there is a job orientation briefing to attend, and then you will meet with supervisory personnel from your specialization and receive your assignment. There is often a need for some additional travel to the field office or shelter where you will be working.

Housing for workers will vary from job to job, depending upon the availability of undamaged hotels with vacancies. On the ARC jobs I have worked thus far, nice, single-occupancy accommodations located about 15 to 20 minutes from my primary work site have been afforded. In one case I was staying in a hotel that had been flooded, but the management had very quickly cleaned up the mess and repaired its damage. Following Hurricane Andrew, on the other hand, there were not enough hotel rooms anywhere near the disaster site. People had to commute long distances to and from work each day and share rooms with other workers.

While you are there, you will work long hours (usually 8:00 a.m. to 6:00 p.m.) and get little, if any, time off. The pace of activity is often rather rapid, so the days tend to fly by. Lunches are often mass care meals served to you in the service centers/ shelters. Before and after the work day, breakfast and supper are often eaten in hotels, restaurants, and fast-food establishments some distance from the disaster area. These meals allow time for fellowship, war stories (tales from previous disasters), and support.

Toward the end of the assignment you will make arrangements to handle close of business (COB) activities such as completing travel vouchers, being given an evaluation of your work, and attending a defusing. Workers are often asked to write a narrative detailing the functions they performed, the numbers and types of interventions they used, and their suggestions as to what worked and what needs to be reworked before next time. You COB through the headquarters office on your last day.

DISASTER MENTAL HEALTH ROLES AND RESPONSIBILITIES WITHIN ARC

Simply stated, the main task of ARC DMH workers is to assist Red Cross workers (paid staff and volunteers), their families, and disaster victims with whatever mental health needs may arise while carrying out on-site disaster assignments. This work involves use of the vast array of interventions being presented throughout this book.

DMH workers can become further involved in ARC by taking additional training courses and then becoming trainers of others who will one day be working in DMH or other ARC specialties. Local and regional Red Cross classes must be offered constantly, in order to maintain readiness levels. Even then, disasters with the scope of the Mississippi River/Midwest floods of 1993 and the Los Angeles earthquake of 1994 required extraordinary, additional efforts. In those disasters, local ARC units were frantically adding extra training classes for newly recruited workers. During the flood, perspective DMH volunteers were being flown to St. Louis for 2 days of intensive DMH training to be followed by immediate field assignments throughout the vast flood zone. Inspired by the Los Angeles earthquake, new DMH recruits were flown to Phoenix for the training and then flown to California and deployed in the Los Angeles area.

The DMH function is still relatively new within ARC. Our role is not always clearly understood by many of the representatives of other specializations. Because we are often given beepers and rental cars, and are free to move about the disaster area in what is largely an autonomous practice, others may get the impression that we are somehow elite. Some staff even seem to fear us, not realizing that we are there, in large part, to help assure their own health and well-being while they are on the job. All of this usually works itself out over time.

ARC is extremely proud of its growing DMH network. National ARC President Elizabeth Dole has often mentioned DMH during interviews stemming from recent, major disasters and the many related fund-raising events. The media frequently seeks out DMH workers to obtain their perspectives on post-disaster recovery issues, and this has been very helpful with public relations, fund-raising, and recruitment.

THE ARC-NASW-APA-ACA-AAMFT PARTNERSHIP

During 1991, ARC signed statements of understanding with the National Association of Social Workers (NASW) and the American Psychological Association (APA) to encourage cooperative efforts between these organizations. More recently, ARC developed similar agreements with the American Counseling Association (ACA) and the American Association of Marriage and Family Therapists (AAMFT).

Members of these organizations have agreed to work with ARC in a variety of areas, including:

- preparedness planning at the local, state, and national levels of the organizations;
- recruitment and training of critically needed human resources — licensed (or credentialed) members who are willing to become DMH volunteers for both local and national assignments; and
- formation of local-level DMH committees that will help coordinate the efforts of these groups.

If you are a member of any one of these groups, or any other professional organizations, you may want to look into how active your local chapter is with ARC and offer your services to help with committee work and local disaster relief.

As you begin your DMH career, you will discover that many of the professional organizations to which you belong have long recognized a professional responsibility to help in times of disaster. The NASW Code of Ethics, for example, directs social workers to "provide appropriate professional services in public emergencies." NASW's National Center for Social Policy and Practice and the Hawaii Chapter of NASW are currently working on a training manual and resource guide to assist social workers who accept a call to disaster service (Lee et al., 1993).

In my community, representatives of several organizations formed a local task force and began having meetings shortly after the cooperation agreements were signed. During our 3 years of operation, we have begun a resource library at our ARC chapter, sponsored training sessions, recruited additional volunteers, assisted with local drills and disasters, and served as a support system for members who have gone out on national jobs. It has been truly refreshing to see so many social workers, psychologists, and counselors working cooperatively with others who are active in local relief efforts.

ARC CHAPTER PINS AND JOB SHIRTS

As a brief side note, I must add that no discussion of ARC would be complete without some mention of ARC pins and shirts—they are a major cultural phenomenon within the organization. Many ARC chapters have designed collector pins that can be worn on clothing, hats, and so on. Be sure to get some of them before they send you out on an assignment, because many of the volunteers you meet at the job will want to trade pins. This is generally done as a one-for-one trade, but some of the fancier ones may cost a few dollars. I was caught short on my first job. In the rush to get me off to the disaster, no one had briefed me on pins.

Job shirts are another ARC staple. Major disasters prompt the design of T-shirts imprinted with the ARC job number (e.g., DR 169), a picture to signify the job (e.g., a Mississippi River flood scene), and enough wording to refresh tired memories years later. They are sold at very reasonable prices to anxious ARC collectors. Because the mode of dress for most disaster workers is casual, they can be put to immediate, practical use.

Watching for pins and for job shirts from previous disasters becomes part of the routine at each new assignment, and workers are very proud of these items. Even if you are not generally interested in such things, it is important for you to be aware of how large a part of the ARC culture they are and be careful not to inadvertently offend someone who is a collector.

VOLUNTEER ORGANIZATIONS
ACTIVE IN DISASTER RELIEF

Besides ARC, there are many other groups of volunteers that are involved in disaster work. So many, in fact, that they have organized into state and national level organizations called Voluntary Organizations Active in Disaster (VOAD). National VOAD (NVOAD) currently includes these groups:

Adventist Community Services
American Radio Relay League, Inc.
American Red Cross
Ananda Marga Universal Relief Team
Catholic Charities USA
Christian Disaster Response, AECCGC
Christian Reformed World Relief Committee
Church of the Brethren
Church World Service
The Episcopal Church
Friends Disaster Service
Inter-Lutheran Disaster Response
Mennonite Disaster Service
Presbyterian Church USA
REACT International, Inc.
The Salvation Army
Society of St. Vincent de Paul
Southern Baptist Convention
United Methodist Church Committee on Relief
Volunteers of America

NVOAD's purpose is to bring together representatives of these organizations in order to foster cooperation, coordination, education, mitigation, and national and regional meetings. They are heavily involved in planning. Working as a volunteer with any of these groups can provide additional DMH experiences.

While doing background research for this book, I attended a Pennsylvania VOAD meeting. That group is convened quarterly by (Pennsylvania's EMA) PEMA in order to improve disaster preparedness in our state. The agenda for that October 27, 1993, meeting included a review of VOAD member organizations' activities in relation to the 1993 Mississippi/Midwest floods; a look at summer of 1993 heat wave deaths that occurred in Philadelphia (117 people died in a 1-week period), as both PEMA and VOAD were looking at ways to prevent a recurrence; efforts to develop a system to use local animal shelters to house pets whenever their owners are displaced by disasters (seeing-eye dogs are about the only animals allowed in shelters); and plans to generate policies that would allow administrative leave time for state employees whose services were needed by VOAD organizations in times of disaster.

After the meeting, I was given a tour of the PEMA Emergency Operations Center (EOC), or control room, from which any disasters can be monitored on several computers and large projection television screens. On one of those screens, staff members were able to watch live CNN coverage of the massive wildfires in southern California. Much to my surprise, on another screen they were following a large and potentially disastrous fuel spill that had occurred in the Lehigh Valley (my home community) during our meeting.

Someone had accidentally dug into a pipeline. Nearly 5,000 people lived and worked in the area, and the Red Cross had already opened a shelter in a school located a safe distance from the spill. Fortunately, it was contained quickly, no one was seriously injured, and the shelter needed to be open only for a few hours. The event gave me quite a memorable visit to PEMA's EOC and VOAD and serves as yet another reminder that disasters can happen any place and any time.

OTHER DMH OPPORTUNITIES —
PROFIT AND NONPROFIT

So far, the options discussed have all been for volunteer work. Other DMH opportunities that can generate income do exist, both for direct service and for consulting. The most obvious is to open your practice to include provision of traditional diagnostic and treatment services to victims who are experiencing worse than normal difficulties as a result of a disaster. Ethically speaking, this should not be done with anyone you have met through volunteer DMH work; unless you plan to see the individuals without charging them for your services, those individuals should be referred elsewhere.

Many small, local fires, chemical spills, violent crimes, transportation wrecks, industrial accidents, and similar catastrophes occur near you each day. The plight of the victims of small disasters is just as real as that from major events. Also, primary and secondary victims of major disasters can appear in your practice even if you are thousands of miles from the point of impact. Many seriously traumatized persons relocate rather than rebuild, thinking that will end their pain. If only it were that easy.

Secondary victims (friends and relatives some distance from the disaster) often suffer along with the primary victims. Sometimes, people quite far from a disaster, who are totally uninvolved with it, will even suffer a stress reaction. Butcher and Hatcher (1988) write that this is especially true in the case of airplane crashes, which often cause a strong *irradiation effect*. Also, the individuals who never fully recovered from previous disasters often suffer with *anniversary reactions* (renewed occurrence of symptoms at the anniversaries of the event) and PTSD. Making others aware of your interest in DMH will help generate referrals.

Teaching about DMH is an option. You can develop and offer workshops and seminars to interested groups of emergency responders. You can also offer elective courses to undergraduate and graduate students preparing to enter mental health-related careers. As a former member of the adjunct faculty of both a community college and a graduate school of social work, I will avoid the temptation to comment upon whether part-time teaching is a profit-making venture.

Carving out a role as a DMH researcher is another idea. Researchers affiliated with various agencies, hospitals, and universities around the country are continuing to explore issues in the areas of prevention, intervention, diagnosis, and treatment of the types of syndromes and illnesses that may develop as a result of exposure to traumatic stress. Grants from CMHS's Violence and Traumatic Stress Research Branch help fund many of these projects.

Another possibility is consulting with business and industry about DMH concerns. A colleague of mine works for a local family service agency which offers post-disaster intervention services to companies on a contractual basis. They work with employees who have witnessed events such as bank robberies, industrial accidents resulting in deaths, and suicides.

Larger corporations may get into psychological damage control, in areas such as public relations and marketing, when issues like product tampering or a huge accident arise. Airlines, for example, have developed *go teams* or *strike forces* to deal with the psychological aftermath of airplane crashes (Frederick, 1981). In many cases, they have done so at the urging of their insurance carriers, because "neurosis claims" lawsuits routinely result in large monetary settlements being awarded to survivors and families of victims who were killed.

Writing can be an option, too. Whether you generate a piece for a professional journal, write a freelance magazine article, or author a book, it allows you to combine elements of teaching and cathartic self-expression. How much you write, and for whom you write, will determine profitability.

It is also possible to find regular DMH-related employment opportunities with ARC, within other VOAD organizations, with FEMA (or other EMAs), or in other agencies, groups, and organizations. The Veteran's Administration has many workers who specialize in treating PTSD; they have the largest PTSD program in the country, and they provide backup to the Department of Defense. The various branches of the military have special units that are working to try to prevent stress responses from ever developing into PTSD. The Navy, for example, has formed SPRINT units, which are CISD teams consisting of social workers, psychologists, psychiatrists, nurses, psych techs, and chaplains.

Chapter 8

THE HELPING PROCESS

DMH utilizes many fundamental helping processes that are routinely taught to students entering fields such as social work, psychology, counseling, nursing, pastoral care, and medicine. Parad et al. (1975a, 1975b), Farberow (1978a, 1978d), Frederick (1981), Farberow and Gordon (1981), and others review the important interviewing and CI techniques that will be summarized in the next few paragraphs.

INTERVIEWING/COUNSELING BASICS

All approaches tend to begin from a conversational base that heavily utilizes active listening skills. The best way to make people aware of your interest and concern is by attending to what is being said. Use reflection, paraphrase, and ask open-ended questions that will draw out more detail about the things people have mentioned. Establish eye contact, be empathetic, and validate the feelings others are expressing.

When speaking, be both self-assured and reassuring in your comments and your delivery. Try to vary your voice tone and inflection. Clarify what others are saying, in order to focus your attention, and check your perceptions of what is being said against the comments' intended meanings. Be hopeful and encouraging, and stress how resilient the human spirit can be. Take your time when starting a conversation. Use small words and phrases at first until you have established that the persons to whom you are speaking are properly able to understand your questions and assimilate the information you have to offer. Remember, if others are still in shock, their thinking will be slowed and rather concrete. They may become lost in conversations they formerly would have easily understood.

It is okay to vary your own mood to fit the circumstances. Many survivors (and other relief workers) enjoy having a bit of humor mixed into these otherwise somber conversations. They also can handle it if you end up crying with them in response to some touching aspect of their story. In fact, sometimes having a good, cleansing cry is the best move for everyone.

Toward the end of the conversation, it is always good to summarize what each person has been saying as a final check that things were being properly understood. Some people may need help in interpreting bits of the conversation. Providing that clarification becomes a valued part of the overall psychoeducational process.

Be certain to assure confidentiality and protect privacy for those you are interviewing. In some circumstances, such as when working with people in a crowd at a service center waiting line, this may not be so important. But, for more formal interviews, defusing, and debriefing, it is critical. Finding a private spot, even if it means taking a walk or sitting in a car, can make a big difference in the effectiveness of certain interventions.

Remember to be aware of issues of diversity when interviewing. Cultural differences can even account for behaviors you might otherwise suspect are warning signs of mental illness. Two prime examples are establishing eye contact (which some cultures view as being insolent) and maintaining personal space/distance (some cultures commonly stand very close). Another example is shaking hands when meeting someone. Although common to many of us, it is replaced by a bow or some other gesture of respect in some cultures.

EMOTIONAL FIRST AID

Many DMH interventions will be very brief contacts, often in the range of 5 to 15 minutes. Although they may be short, they are often high in emotional content. They can be extremely effective in lowering stress levels, providing education about mental health-related issues, and allowing time to screen large numbers of victims and staff for signs of more serious concerns.

Regardless of whether the sessions are of short or long duration, basic conversational skills and use of self, the often automatic responses of both natural helpers and trained workers, can have a major, positive impact upon people in crisis. Here are some helpful hints:

1. **Remain Calm—Be an Appropriate Role Model.** Do not allow the client or the stressful situation to make you lose your cool, or you will quickly become an ineffective helper.

2. **Introduce Yourself and Your Agency/Services Role.** Let people know who you are and what role you are playing in the relief operation. As noted earlier, it is sometimes better to put a bit of a spin on the role definition and say that your primary role is to assist victims and staff with crisis intervention or stress management.

3. **Get Needed Demographic Information Immediately.** Do this before getting into the details of the problems and issues each person is facing. Starting off with a few basic questions aimed at gathering names, addresses, and phone numbers can be very helpful with calming and focusing the people being interviewed. It also is critical to get that information immediately when handling telephone crises in case the person hangs up or accidentally gets disconnected.

4. **Use Active Listening Skills and Allow Plenty of Time for Ventilation.** These points cannot be stressed enough. People under stress will benefit from spending some of their nervous energy telling (and retelling) their stories. You can help the most and, simultaneously, learn what you need to know about them, by letting them do most of the talking. Even young children probably can tell you their stories. Many children will express themselves verbally; others will share their feelings via their drawings and/or their play.

5. **Giving Process Details Helps Lessen Fear of the Unknown.** Once the person you are interviewing has had a chance to ventilate, the time is right for you to provide simple, factual information about the physical and emotional aspects of their story that are DMH related. Simply reassuring folks that what they are experiencing is normal for persons under severe stress, giving them the most basic pointers on stress management, and alerting them to some of the ups and downs that are yet to come will greatly boost their spirits. It will

also help inoculate them against further stress and provide them additional mental energy to move forward in their recovery.

Lots of good, written, educational material is quickly available in pamphlet form at major disaster scenes. There are even therapeutic coloring books about common events like floods, earthquakes, and tornadoes. Although these are targeted primarily for use with children, I have found that older siblings, parents, and grandparents can benefit from these resources as they explore them with the youngsters. Hand these out, but also take a few minutes to highlight the critical sections that are most relevant for each person's situation.

6. **Be Truthful About What You Have to Offer and Be Careful Not to Overstate It.** Whenever possible, give people honest answers, rather than platitudes. Openness and honesty are needed with children too. Although young people may not fully understand everything that is said to them, they can usually read and judge feelings better than many adults; they know when they are being snowed by others (given information that is not truthful) and they do not appreciate it.

Sometimes, however, a measured response may be best. A good example might be an emergency room worker telling a seriously injured auto accident victim that others in the car "were seriously injured but we're doing everything we can . . .," rather than immediately hitting him or her with the brutal truth that the others did not survive at a time when that total honesty may cause the person to go into shock.

Kindler, Duncan, and Knapp (1991) offer another good example. In their brief article, they detail the Pennsylvania Psychological Association's efforts to help the survivors of the helicopter and plane collision that killed Senator Heinz and several others (including young children) when the wreckage landed in an elementary school playground. The disaster response team's primary goal was to make a group of helpers available to form a *safety net* for those who might need and seek services.

In doing so, and in publicizing their availability, they were careful to show "concern for the vulnerability of the survivors . . . [and they] did not attempt to solicit victims or families with predictions of long-term mental health consequences." They point out that, by carelessly making an overly direct appeal of that sort, their efforts "might increase anxiety among the effected population," and result in more negative overall outcomes (pp. 15-17).

7. **Verify Attentiveness.** People in crisis are often in shock, to some degree. Depending upon where they are in the time line of recovery, they may also be rather angry. Either way, they may not be fully attending to (or comprehending) conversations. Workers may need to repeat things several times in an interview. Sometimes you will catch someone on a bad day, and you will need to go over everything again on another day. It is always a good idea to provide the same information to several members of the same family (or to a group of friends). That way, at least one of them will probably understand and remember the material.

8. **Usually, It Is Best Not to Stop Any Tears.** This is another point that bears repeating. A helper's first impulse might be to get the person to stop crying and regain composure. Instead, get the person a tissue and allow time for a good, cleansing cry. It is also natural and common for workers to sometimes need to cry with someone after hearing what he or she has just been through.

9. **Sometimes, Giving a Hug May Help.** Touching has long been a part of comforting. Sometimes it is appropriate. Other times the person in crisis may become more upset if you violate his or her personal space. Judge for yourself if holding someone's hand, patting someone on the back, or giving a hug fits the situation and your personal style.

10. **Shun "Superman/Wonderwoman" Urges and Involve Others.** Discover or develop support systems for the persons with whom you are working and do the same for yourself. There is a great deal of work to be done in

the wake of a disaster, and no one person can handle
everything. Help others realize that, unless they want
to experience burnout, they must get into the habit of
sharing the stress and the tasks of recovery among as
many people as possible.

11. **Learn to Recognize and Remember Your Own Limitations.** Persons in crisis cannot always accomplish everything they would like to do or cope with every situation they might encounter. Still, people tend to feel
and report things like "I should have been able to handle
this." We all have different tolerances for the events
we encounter in everyday life. Some might enjoy working with children, while others prefer the elderly. Some
can easily handle work with those who have just lost
family members, while others need to avoid those issues (possibly due to an unresolved loss of their own).
The simple fact is that sometimes it is best to turn down
situations that are too emotionally charged to allow you
to handle them effectively.

DISASTER MENTAL HEALTH
CRISIS INTERVENTION (CI)

The next step beyond providing emotional first aid often involves CI. Three important DMH objectives at this point in the
helping process are:

1. To relieve feelings of survivor (or helper) anxiety, depression, and guilt.
2. To prevent further disorganization or decompensation.
3. To screen for those persons with more serious problems
and/or issues who may require additional services (and
possibly need ongoing mental health treatment).

For most DMH interventions, there is also a simple, three-part
formula for success:

1. **Get People Talking.** Explore disaster issues and target
questions to areas of loss. Delve into tangible (objective)
losses of people and property, but also look into the sym-
bolic (subjective) meanings of those losses. Perception

seems to wield the same power as reality when it comes to triggering stress reactions and their long-term consequences.

During moments of reflection, the traumatic events people have experienced will be revivified. Be their guide-wire or safety-line to the present. When needed, however, bring them back from their negative memories and reassure them that the worst is over and they are safe now. Excessive reflection on tragedy can work against recovery. A study by Nolen-Hoeksema and Morrow (1991) found that victims who were focused on their symptoms and negative emotions remained symptomatic longer than those who displayed less rumination and more distracting responses (e.g., talking about going places or doing things with friends).

Try to spend some time talking about those aspects of life that have not been changed by the disaster. These things can often be used as strengths upon which to rebuild a base of emotional stability. In doing this you may also encounter things that have been changed for the better, as people have discovered and drawn upon some inner reserves or external supports that they may not have previously recognized they had available to them.

2. **Get People Busy.** Focused activities move people beyond shock and into recovery, so get folks doing something constructive. If they have not already done so, encourage them to return to the disaster site and begin to process their feelings about the event. Go with them if you have to, in order to get them there. Have them begin to salvage whatever they can save. Get them to apply for available aid or to submit their insurance claims. Have them reestablish a residence and replace key items like clothing, food, beds, and appliances. They may need to plan for a funeral.

Children can be assigned tasks, too. Helping clean up, running errands, drawing or painting scenes from the disaster (or working in therapeutic coloring books), playing with younger children, entertaining elderly persons who may not have anything to do, or any similar activities are fine. Persons housed in shelters can ease some of their stress by helping with cooking, cleaning, and other shelter chores.

What people are doing is not as important as the fact that they are doing something. Working in Florida after a coastal flood, I once met a man in his late 70s whose beachfront trailer was torn in half by the storm. Much of the contents had washed away. He and his wife were planning to rebuild. Despite poor health, he was there, raking and sifting the sand, keeping aside whatever he found that was usable. His wife was too frail to work beside him, but, each evening, he would share his treasures with her. At one point he found and proudly showed me a Mickey Mouse spoon his children had once enjoyed using. This was his therapy.

3. **Begin Problem Solving.** Helping victims get a handle on some issues, however small, establishes a firm foundation that will help them regain a sense of self-assurance and control over their own lives. Once a DMH intervention has jump-started this part of the healing process, problem-solving ability will usually take off on its own.

   Always remember, however, that the on-scene DMH program is only meant to provide brief interventions; it is not meant to become therapy. No more than three sessions should be needed to provide preventive educational material, screen for more serious difficulties, and make any needed referrals.

THE MIRACULOUS HEALING POWERS OF SLEEP

Sleep, or the lack of it, can be a DMH worker's best friend or worst enemy. Sometimes you will be talking with individuals (victims or workers) who seem to be thoroughly down and depressed. You will wonder how are they ever going to go on with the work of recovery. Then, a day or so later, you will see them again, now appearing more active, upbeat, and aggressively fighting those recovery battles. The difference is often as simple as one or two good nights of sleep.

Sleep deprivation can easily result from the many stresses that are generated by the disaster. Before long, it leaves people feeling tired and poorly motivated to get on with their lives. Fortunately, most will give in to natural urges and get needed rest before serious problems arise. Some people, however, may miss sleep for longer periods of time; for them, more significant difficulties may lie ahead. Prolonged sleep deprivation will often cause mood swings, disorientation, feelings of depersonalization, and similar difficulties, as cognitive functioning is diminished.

Be mindful of your own need for sleep and caution others about it. Be especially aware of persons with any prior history of behavior that might be exacerbated by prolonged disruption in sleep patterns, as often happens with thought disorders, many types of depression, and affective illnesses. Be alert to people who move to the other end of the spectrum and begin sleeping excessively, as that, too, is a warning sign of more serious problems.

DEFUSING

Defusing is the term given to the process of *talking it out*—allowing victims and workers the opportunity to ventilate about their disaster-related memories, stresses, losses, and methods of coping, and to be able to do so in a safe and supportive atmosphere.

The defusing process usually involves informal and impromptu sessions. A DMH worker might witness an emotional interchange between a victim and another staff member and, soon afterward, approach one or both of them and open a dialogue. This will, in turn, help them release thoughts and feelings that might not otherwise be expressed. Suppression or repression of this kind of highly charged material might lead to the development of any number of stress-related physical and/or mental illnesses.

Greeting a victim who is waiting in line at a disaster service center and offering a snack or a drink, or playing a game with a child in an emergency shelter, or making a purchase from a clerk at a store in a disaster area, or even ordering a meal while in the field can be enough of an opportunity to open a dialogue with someone who is anxious to tell his or her story. Running into a coworker at the copy machine offers the same chance. So does going out to eat with other staff members.

My experience is that some folks may require a little coaxing, and some may not be ready to talk about things at all, but most people you encounter will see the DMH worker as someone who is trained and ready to listen. Their stories will begin to pour out, if given even the slightest opportunity to do so.

What can you do to try to make the defusing sessions be positive experiences? Hartsough (1985) and Myers (1985) offer several suggestions:

1. The overall tone should be positive and supportive. Take time and make an effort to recognize the many positive contributions made by those who are present.
2. Avoid criticism of how people behaved or how they felt. People are not always at their best when under pressure, so care needs to be taken not to hurt feelings when offering suggestions for change. Saying something like, "I remember I did the same thing (or felt the same way) on my first assignment; my supervisor talked to me about it and explained . . .," can ease the tension and still convey an important message.
3. Seek out persons who were likely the hardest hit by the event and its aftermath (those who suffered the greatest losses) and try to engage them in a defusing interview. It is also a good idea to invite them to any formal debriefing sessions that may be held. Victims and other staff members who are helping with the relief effort probably can help you identify the individuals who will need to be encouraged to be interviewed.
4. When defusing others, try to keep your own injection of tales from previous disasters (war stories) to a minimum. This is their time to vent and your time to be an active listener. Hearing how well you handled a similar event does little to provide any emotional support or release for the person(s) being defused.
5. On the other hand, do not be surprised to hear war stories from disaster workers about their previous experiences and how they handled things then. Sometimes a

topic is just too emotionally charged for someone to share at the time when it first occurs. Later, given some time to process it, the story, and the related feelings, will often emerge. As an example, serving in Hurricane Andrew apparently was an extremely stressful assignment for many ARC workers. Their stories have continued to pour out in defusings and debriefings held for more recent disasters, even though it has now been a long time since Andrew occurred.

Hartsough (1985) and Myers (1985) also caution DMH workers not to be surprised by the expression of angry feelings during a defusing interview. Anger is a natural emotion at some points during the recovery process. DMH workers need to become comfortable with hearing expressions of angry feelings and, at the same time, realize the anger is not really directed at them (and should not be taken personally). Myers (1994) offers this tip for helping deal with the anger victims will express about the bureaucratic nightmare that disaster relief can be — refer to the problematic aspects of the relief process as "the second disaster" and openly talk about it. By doing so, you will provide some validation and stress-inoculation, and you can often inject a bit of humor into a tense moment.

There are many formats (and lists of questions) that can be used in defusing relief workers. Most of them begin with introductions and a statement about confidentiality. Then, they generally focus most of the sessions on the workers' reviews of the best and the worst aspects of their assignments. Other frequent topics are the stress relief strategies they used, comparisons of the present job to previous assignments, and suggestions for improving future jobs. The sessions usually conclude with a conversation about making the transition from relief workers back to predisaster roles and responsibilities, with special attention to the stresses that will be encountered back home.

Occasionally, someone's experience may seem to have been a totally miserable one. The only stories he or she tells are reflective of disappointment and failure. Before either party ends the interview, try to refocus the person onto something positive, even if you have to look back with him or her to previous disasters or to some aspect of the person's home life. Remind people who are down that they can now leave the negative things behind them as they head for home. It may be worthwhile to offer suggestions for avoiding similar problems on future jobs. Help them begin to put some emotional distance between themselves and the troublesome issues. Stress with them that they are "special" people for doing what they do to help others in times of need.

DEBRIEFING

The debriefing is a formal meeting, generally held 24 to 72 hours after an unusually stressful incident, strictly for the purpose of dealing with the emotional residuals of the event. Any location that is large enough to accommodate the group, and which can be secured so as to assure privacy, is appropriate for use. This session may require a block of time that is several hours in length, particularly if a process such as Mitchell's (1983) formal CISD model is used. More detail about CISD will be provided in the next section of this book.

An atlernative to CISD is the modification known as the *multiple stressor debriefing model* (MSD). Armstrong et al. (1995) explain that this variation was developed for use with workers following a disaster relief operation.

MSD uses abreaction and psychoeducation formatted in four phases: (1) disclosure of events, (2) feelings and reactions, (3) coping strategies, and (4) termination. (p. 84)

The issues that surface during MSD or CISD sessions may not all be resolved during the meeting. Follow-up contacts and peer supports are ofter needed to continue processing the event.

Whenever possible, everyone involved in the crisis should attend the debriefings. Many organizations recommend or even require attending defusing or debriefing sessions whenever certain types of incidents occur. ARC, for instance, offers defusing, as necessary, throughout a person's tour of duty at a disaster scene. ARC also strongly recommends (but does not require) having one before leaving for home. Once ARC workers get home, their local ARC chapter usually offers them a formal debriefing.

Mays (1993) stressed that everyone present at the session needs to be given a chance to talk about his or her experiences in relation to the disaster event and the subsequent recovery efforts, so as to reduce the *conspiracy of silence* that so often exists for some participants. Those present will likely have sights, sounds, smells, tactile memories, and possibly even tastes that trigger negative memories and prompt reactions which they may fear are abnormal. They need to see and hear that others share the same thoughts and feelings.

Abueg, Drescher, and Kubany (1994) discuss the therapeutic value of victim or staff member self-disclosure and note that, "from a behavioral perspective, conditioned avoidance can be minimized through health re-exposure or extinction of feared cues in the context of the trauma"(pp. 242-243). They suggest using implosive therapy to help evoke the details of the traumatic events. This can be done by pursuing three distinct lines of inquiry:

1. **Symptom-Contingent Cues.** Question people about their current disaster-related problems, losses, symptoms, and fears.
2. **Serial or Contextual Cues.** Question what people were getting as sensory input (seeing, hearing, smelling, tasting, and feeling) during the traumatic event.
3. **Psychodynamic Cues.** Question what memories and emotions from previous life trauma where reactivated by the present event; unresolved guilt is commonly a part of the scenarios described by victims.

Talbot (1990) cautions of the potential for *parallel process* issues to arise. During a debriefing, helpers often experience similar feelings, thoughts, and behavior to the ones being expressed by those they are trying to help. Sometimes, these phenomena leave the helpers feeling as hopeless and immobilized as the victims, causing increased stress and a misguided process, rather than healthy ventilation and positive moves toward recovery.

To assure the best chances for success, a debriefing should be conducted by an experienced mental health facilitator, or done by a pair of facilitators. The many directions a session might take, and the strong emotions that so often are expressed, may tend to overwhelm an inexperienced group leader. Having more than one person guide the meeting also allows for better monitoring of audience and facilitator responses, whether spoken or nonverbal.

There should also be one or two trained individuals in reserve near the exits from the room in which the debriefing is done. Sometimes someone will have a strong reaction to something that is said or done, and that person will leave the room. A worker needs to follow him or her out and intervene in order to assess the problem, defuse it, and work to get the person back into the group session.

CRITICAL INCIDENT
STRESS DEBRIEFING (CISD)

The CISD process (Mitchell, 1983) involves an individual or group interview between the emergency responders who witnessed a critical incident and a facilitator (or sometimes several facilitators, depending upon the size of the group). Mitchell lists four types of debriefing: *On-Scene* (or Near-Scene); *Initial Defusing; Formal CISD;* and *Follow-Up CISD.* All allow time for introductions, ventilation, education, screening, and lots of support. The screenings are designed to detect signs of serious stress reactions that might require special attention (additional sessions and/or referral).

On-Scene (or Near-Scene) debriefings and *Initial Defusing* sessions, all of which generally occur in the immediate vicinity of the disaster area, are the shorter and less structured formats and are the ones most frequently used by DMH field workers. The material offered in the preceding pages has already addressed several hints about brief approaches.

Formal CISD sessions are highly structured and tend to require a time commitment of several hours. Mitchell's (1983) format for these meetings involves six phases, each with specific functions: Phase one begins with introductions and a description of process details (especially the need for everyone's assurance of confidentiality). Phase two is a review of factual material about the incident. Phase three is the sharing of feelings stirred by the event. Phase four is a review of symptoms of stress the participants are experiencing. Phase five is the instructional portion of the process, with facilitators teaching about *normal* reactions to stress. Phase six, which occurs during the final moments of the session, is used for bringing about closure to the process and looking ahead to any future needs of the group.

Follow-Up CISD sessions are optional, depending upon the needs of the group. If held, they may occur weeks or even months later, usually in an effort to resolve any issues which still are troubling the group. They are, according to Mitchell (1983), similar to an ongoing therapy process, and they are the hardest of the four types of CISD to successfully perform.

Because I had not yet had formal training in the Mitchell model, I called upon an associate of mine with the local ARC DMH group, who has served as part of a CISD team on 12 or so occasions, to offer a few of his observations (Jeff Kindler, personal communication, December 5, 1993). These are his comments:

> The debriefing process, while rather standardized, requires a degree of flexibility in order to encourage group process. The usual procedure is to establish the norms for the group (e.g., confidentiality) and then recreate the scene using the various roles and experiences of each [individual].
>
> Recreating the scene can be like a play with several subplots emerging, as the various [individuals or subgroup members] share what had happened to them or to [others who were present]. For example, in one situation, a fireman became distressed because he, while usually first on the scene, was second in a multi-casualty vehicular fire. This placed him in a role he was less accustomed to [handling], resulting in feelings of guilt. He wished he had been more helpful. [At the same session] another worker expressed feelings of inadequacy in regard to how she had handled a histrionic witness.
>
> After establishing the facts, the CISD session moves sequentially through the thought, reaction, and symptom phases, which roughly translate into cognitive, affective, and behavioral processing. It is [at this point]

when flexibility may be most important. On the one hand, the debriefer strives to guide the group through each of the phases to complete the process [as outlined by Mitchell]. On the other hand, each [debriefing team] member has a professional style which emphasizes, to a greater or lesser extent, the cognitive, affective, or behavioral [elements]. Thus, debriefing requires [making] allowance for each [team] member's [preferred therapeutic and coping] style.

In terms of the debriefing team, it should include a mental health professional as the team leader and, ideally, two or more emergency responders [e.g., other relief workers] who are also trained as peer support personnel. They must come from a unit that was not involved at [exactly] the same incident . . . [but, because they have had similar experiences] they are easily accepted and will serve as a bridge to help the team leader understand [and communicate with] the emergency workers [who are being debriefed].

Robinson and Mitchell (1993) have found that debriefing has a positive effect upon workers who experienced a stress response after handling critical incidents. They studied a large group of emergency responders and found:

The positive impact and value of debriefing on personnel was marked. Most personnel who reported symptoms of stress . . . stated that these had been reduced as a consequence of attending the debriefing. Further, the greater the impact of an event on staff, the greater was the rated value of the debriefing. (p. 380)

They go on to report that their study left them with a broader understanding of one of the primary mechanisms of the CISD process — talking with others who have experienced the same (or similar) situations:

Talking can, in itself, lead to articulation of thoughts and emotions so that the person has a better understanding and control over his or her internal processes, especially emotions and disturbing cognitions. It may be the case that the emotion that is dissociated or "put on hold" during an emergency or crisis is able to be united in a holistic sense during discussion, and that this is satisfying and therapeutic in terms of the person "coming to terms" with the trauma. (p. 380)

Anyone interested in joining a CISD team should contact any of the various emergency responders in their area to explore if there is a local team and, if so, how to contact one of its members. In the event that there is not one nearby, others from teams in neighboring areas are generally more than happy to assist with getting a team going. Once connected with a team, you will receive training in the full details of the Mitchell model. Then, you will likely get called upon to help facilitate debriefings in or near your home area.

POST-TRAUMATIC
STRESS DISORDER (PTSD)

The development of PTSD is an all-too-common result of exposure to the unusually severe stress events encompassed in disasters and post-disaster recovery. Carson and Butcher (1992) list these five common symptoms of the disorder:

1. The traumatic event is persistently reexperienced via recurrent, intrusive thoughts and/or nightmares.
2. Victims attempt to avoid anything that might result in an association to the traumatic event, so as to avoid further related stress, anxiety, sadness, and pain.
3. Chronic tension, insomnia, and/or a heightened sense of arousal leaves victims feeling that they simply can never relax.
4. Victims experience difficulties with concentration and memory impairment.
5. Depressive symptoms occur, especially social isolation, loss of sexual interest, and general avoidance of anything that might cause excitement (which would then generate more stress). (p. 156)

When these symptoms have lasted for at least 1 month, and have occurred within the first 6 months following the precipitating event, the condition is considered to be an *acute* reaction. If it falls after the 6-month window, it is called a *delayed* reaction.

Mays (1993) pointed out that the Army's first-responders did not care for the notion of calling this condition PTSD because of the "disorder" label, and because there were often signs that occurred before the 1st month anniversary of the disaster. Instead, those in the Army prefer to call it a Post-Traumatic Stress Reaction (PTSR). They feel the term "reaction" is not as pejorative and it better implies normalcy and expectations for recovery. Mays listed the immediate interventions used in the military: rest, replenishment, respite, and reassurance.

The debate (and related research) continues within the mental health field as to why there is an emergence of PTSD in some but not all victims. Is it a result of a biological predisposition, compromised predisaster physiology, premorbid personality type, prior learning and patterns of coping, or maybe some combination and interplay of all of these? Or, is it just a typical reaction that anyone could have, given the same exposure to high levels of stress? So far, Abueg et al. (1994) note that "one relatively consistent finding" in studies of disaster stress "is the dose-response relationship between traumatic exposure and the development of PTSD" (p. 239) — there appears to be good evidence of dose dependency playing a major role.

Whatever the causal factors may be, the treatments are the same. Encourage ventilation, provide therapeutic supports (usually a combination of social supports and psychotherapy), and have the person get enough rest. Sometimes sedation is necessary to allow victims to get the rest they need. In fact, in Vietnam, soldiers were sometimes given *sleep therapy*, enough chlorpromazine (1,000-1,500 mg. per day) to heavily sedate them for 72 hours, in order to initiate their recovery (Freedman et al., 1972).

Severe cases will require referral for ongoing services. Cognitive-behavioral therapy (Dattilio & Freeman, 1994), psychoeducational approaches, hypnosis, support groups, relaxation techniques, writing about the experiences (for personal/therapeutic reasons and/or for publication), art therapy, and play therapy have all proven effective with some victims. So, too, has neurolinguistic programming (Garrison, 1986; Garrison et al., 1993) and psychodrama (Tecala, 1993).

Workers are also susceptible to developing PTSD. It is one of the all-too-common risks for emergency workers, especially the first responders and those at the front lines. Bille (1993) describes the lengthy struggle he has had to overcome a battle with PTSD (and a related battle with alcoholism) stemming from his service as a nurse in Vietnam. He notes the futility of trying to hold things inside or mask problems with addictive behavior. After many years, and despite his recovery efforts, there are still triggers that stir disquieting feelings within him, such as when he viewed news coverage of Operation Desert Storm.

For Vietnam veterans, the smells of oriental cooking or of burning diesel fuel, the sounds of fireworks, cars backfiring, or helicopters, or other similar stimuli can trigger the haunting memories all over again (Sherwood, 1991). I recently was told about a relief worker who was serving on Kauai following Hurricane Iniki. She was talking on the phone to her husband back home one day. He heard helicopters in the background on her end of the call; they were ferrying relief supplies to the island. That sound triggered a Vietnam-related traumatic response in him that was so severe that she had to return home.

From a prevention point of view, workers always need to pay careful attention to their own needs and the needs of their coworkers so that PTSD can be averted whenever possible. An upcoming section is devoted to the topic of stress management.

MENTAL STATUS EXAMS

For some individuals, a concrete approach will not be enough. The disaster-related stressors and/or an obsessive review of the disaster events will cause (or surface) serious difficulties. When more extensive psychopathology is evident, Parad et al. (1975a) recommend using a formal mental status examination to gather a more thorough picture. The typical components of the mental status exam involve assessment of:

- *Appearance*—physical characteristics, clothing, and personal hygiene.
- *Behavior*—posture, expressions, body language, speech quality and volume, and relationship with the interviewer.
- *Affect and Mood*—feelings and their appropriateness.

- *Perception*—presence of hallucinations or illusions.
- *Thinking*—intellectual functioning, orientation (to person, place, and time), insight, judgment, memory (immediate, recent, and remote), thought content (obsessions, compulsions, phobias, suicidal or homicidal ideation, delusions, etc.), and stream of thought (as displayed in speech).

If you take a moment and look back over some of the descriptions of victims that can be found in the first sections of the chapter entitled "Development and Evolution of Disaster Mental Health Strategies" (Chapter 4), you will see that those characterizations encompassed many aspects of a mental status exam.

Once you have acquired a better grasp for a person's specific problems and needs, you can make appropriate referrals accordingly. Upon entering a DMH job, familiarize yourself with local mental health treatment resources (public and private), commitment laws/regulations, and crisis hotlines. Supervisors will generally prepare lists of this kind of information when they first arrive on the job. If this has not been done, contact the local community mental health center and/or professional groups. Then, when more difficult cases emerge, you will be ready to make referrals directly to key contact persons in the receiving agencies, or to take whatever other emergency steps may be necessary in order to assure everyone's safety.

Some readers who do not come from CI or emergency mental health backgrounds may still feel uncomfortable about working with clients who are showing signs of severe stress and, possibly, more serious forms of mental illness. The sections that follow will describe this in more detail, further exploring aspects of the interviewing process and delving more deeply into screening issues and determination of suicidal risk.

THE CONTROLLED
INTERVIEW PROCESS

Many people are fearful of other persons whom they perceive to have a serious form of psychopathology. The strong stigma of mental illness is such that many still incorrectly believe that the illness directly equates to danger. I recently served as a consultant to a group of volunteer coordinators—individuals who reported having little or no experience in working with those afflicted with any type of mental illness. I found that they would often react with fear (and sometimes would panic) when interviewing someone who was mentally ill. Consequently, whatever interviewing skills and/or game plan that they ordinarily would have used for handling tough cases were lost to them because of their own stress response.

To help the interviewers refocus, to advance them beyond their initial fear, and to enable them to effectively interview and serve even those clients who had initially frightened them, I developed a rather simple *controlled interview process* (Weaver, 1993b). Although this procedure was originally designed for volunteer coordinators, I have since found it to be helpful with other, potentially stressful interviews. It is especially useful when confronted by individuals who are hostile and angry.

The following tips are adapted from that process, and may be helpful in any interview situations that might be creating tension:

1. **Take your time and deliver all of your actions and comments more slowly and deliberately than usual.** Violations of this first and very simple concept can raise everyone's level of anxiety and may worsen the interview climate.

2. **Do not allow anyone to make you "blow your cool"** (lose your composure). By remaining calm and not raising your voice when confronted, you are beginning to regain control of the interview from the other person.

3. **Gather some demographic information** (e.g., name and address) **and verify attentiveness**. As noted in an earlier section, this is important material to have available. The main reason you are asking for it now, however, has more to do with its calming effects. It will help greatly in refocusing both the individual and the interview climate to conditions conducive of a better overall mood among all parties.

4. **If you are blessed with a quick wit and a low-key, nonthreatening sense of humor, use it.** Humor can be effective in helping break the tension of a stressful moment. Be careful, though, never to make a comment that

might cause the individual to think you are making fun of (or belittling) him or her. Instead, poke a little fun at yourself for something you said (or did, or need to do), for example. This will show your gentle, human frailty and will lessen any threat the other person may feel from you. Believe it or not, he or she is probably more anxious and fearful about this than you are—many times you are just too upset or scared to notice it.

5. **Do not accept pushy, demanding behavior.** Unless you are very comfortable with the person (and the overall situation), firmly tell him or her you will schedule an appointment to continue at a later time (when you will be more mentally prepared, or when more workers are available to provide some additional security). Schedule that session before parting. Remember, if you do not have enough time for a good intervention, or if you are in the wrong frame of mind, you will not be of much help. Explain that to the other person and reschedule.

6. **Explore feelings and motivation by doing a detailed interview.** It takes time, but it really gives you a better sense for what the person wants and needs. It also allows ventilation, which will lower tension. This interview may also result in discovering that the person has come to the wrong place altogether. If the services he or she is seeking are available elsewhere, a simple referral may happily resolve the matter for everyone.

7. **Further test motivation and begin moving toward problem resolution by assigning one or two small tasks.** Having the person return for a scheduled appointment (as suggested in Step #5) is one exceptionally good way to do this. This gives everyone time to calm down and, as time passes, added perspective becomes available. You might ask the person to gather some documents needed to file a claim, have the person draft a letter, or do anything else that will buy you some time to regroup and, also, help move the person in the right direction.

8. **Get consent and release forms signed and gather more background information.** This is often needed for making any necessary referrals, or to be able to relay infor-

mation to the person's current therapist, physician, and so on. If possible, and besides written information, try to phone some of these contacts in order to get supplementary, off-the-record impressions.

9. **Praise the person for opening up and sharing information about whatever problems and needs he or she has revealed.** Although his or her efforts to seek help may sometimes seem to be awkward, doing so probably has been a major step for that person, as it is for many troubled individuals. People need to be given acceptance and support for having admitted they have a problem that they cannot resolve on their own.

10. **Explore the person's support system, do a strengths-based assessment of the individual, and use both the strengths and the supports to your advantage.** This may include involving family members, friends, caseworkers, members of the clergy, treatment professionals, and/or representatives of various self-help and advocacy groups in planning to assist with the person's recovery.

11. **Try not to say "NO" and never deceive the person.** Instead, take the time to openly and honestly explain why something he or she wants may not be possible.

12. **Never make statements you cannot substantiate or promises you cannot keep.** Saying "I don't know, but I'll try to find out," is a better response than one that will later turn out to be incorrect. Everyone can easily recall the statements made to us by others that caused us to experience feelings of disappointment and hurt.

13. **Write reminder notes regarding the tough (or unusual) interviews**. People tend to sometimes hear and remember only what they like to (or want to) hear and disregard the rest. The best ways to avoid communication problems are to:

    • have the other person keep written reminders of all assigned tasks, appointments, names, dates, times, and so on.
    • keep your own summary notes about each visit, so you can keep track of what was said by all parties, what

tasks were assigned, any unusual statements or behavior, and what (if any) commitments you made to
the individual.

This way, you probably can easily pick up the process
the next time you have contact with the person (or with
others in the person's behalf). Notes in the person's
record should simply and factually describe the events
that occurred. Be careful not to use words that document negative value judgments or opinions. A good
rule of thumb is: *Do not write anything you would
not want used against you in court.*

This process can be used to add a bit of formal (yet passive)
structure to any difficult interview. Just by maintaining this
unpretentious form of control, and by avoiding an overt power
struggle with the person you are trying to interview, you can
avoid victimization by someone who is prone to being pushy or
demanding. When used in combination with the other elements
of DMH, the controlled interview process can be an extremely
effective tool.

SCREENING ISSUES

The following material should help clarify some types of information that often must be gathered while screening persons
in crisis. This kind of data will also help you decide whom you
can help with short-term interventions and who is in such serious need for treatment that they may require an immediate referral to other sources of emergency care, such as the community mental health clinic, a local professional who provides the
person's regular treatment, the nearest emergency room, or the
local crisis intervention team.

1. **What drew special attention to this person?**
2. **What are the person's presenting problems?** Try to obtain all of the various perspectives — those of the person,
   the person's family, the referral source, and so on.
3. **How long have the problems existed?** Did they precede
   the current crisis?

4. **What help (support, education, or treatment services) has the person received and from whom?** Did that help seem to be effective?

5. **What medications, prescription and nonprescription (or over-the-counter), are being used by the person for physical conditions?** Type and dosage, number of pills or amount of liquid remaining, side effects, and so on, for nonpsychiatric medical conditions. In order to provide you with some rationale as to why this is important, here is a partial list of drugs that will sometimes cause symptoms of depression as a side effect:

   - antihypertensives (e.g., Methyldopa, Propranolol, and Clonidine)
   - antiparkinsonian agents (e.g., Carbidopa-Levodopa and Amantadine)
   - hormones (e.g., Estrogen and Progesterone)
   - corticosteroids (e.g., Cortisone Acetate and Cortone)
   - anticancer agents (e.g., Vincristine and Vinblastine)

   Other medications may cause symptoms that mimic other forms of mental illness, including anxiety symptoms and even psychosis.

6. **What medications, if any, is the person taking for any psychiatric condition(s) for which he or she is receiving treatment?** Appendix A (pp. 171-173) is a reference listing of commonly used psychotropic medications (with both brand names and generic names), sorted by their functions (antidepressant, antipsychotic, etc.). If the person is not currently medicated, have medications been used, successfully or unsuccessfully, in the past?

7. **Is the person self-medicating (abusing street drugs, alcohol, prescription drugs, and/or nonprescription medications)?** If so, a substance abuse evaluation (and treatment) may be needed before other types of intervention.

8. **Has the person had a good, recent physical examination to rule out any physical problems that might be causing the current difficulties?** Here is a partial list of diseases and organic disorders that are associated with symptoms of depression:

arteriosclerosis	malignancies
asthma	metabolic problems
autoimmune disorders	multiple sclerosis
cardiovascular disorders	neurologic disorders
diabetes mellitus	pernicious anemia
endocrine disorders	rheumatoid arthritis
idiopathic parkinsonism	syphilis
infectious hepatitis	ulcerative colitis
influenza	uremia
lupus	vitamin deficiencies

Similar to the situation with medications, these and other physical conditions might generate symptoms that mimic other types of mental illness. Involve medical professionals whenever medication problems or medical conditions are evident.

9. **Is there a family history of mental illness?** If so, what treatments were used/effective? What is the family's attitude about going for treatment?

10. **What changes in mood, behavior, sleep, appetite, ability to concentrate, motivation, and so on, are present?** Do they appear to be disaster related or did the changes predate the disaster?

11. **If depression is mentioned (or seems obvious), ask about current (and previous) thoughts of suicide and/or attempts.** If suicide was ever attempted, how lethal was the means? Is there any history of family members or friends having taken their own lives? An upcoming section will offer many more tips on screening persons whom you suspect might be suicidal.

12. **If anger and/or poor impulse control are issues, explore thoughts (and history of actions) of harming self or others.** If you are worried about someone but not quite sure of their potential dangerousness, get a second worker to pair up with you for the interview. In cases like these, it is helpful to have ready access to a second opinion from another DMH specialist or from local professionals.

13. **If the person is hearing voices, displays suspiciousness of others, sees things, feels odd sensations, believes**

he or she is being controlled by others or by the media, and so on, these are often good indicators of serious illness. Be aware, though, that medication reactions, high fevers, and even excessive sleep loss can cause transient episodes of psychosis.

It is always a good idea to conclude any detailed screening interview with a general, open-ended question that will allow the individual to fill in any gaps. Say something like, "Is there anything I did not ask you that might be important for me to know about how things are going with you since the disaster?" DMH workers who are not involved in a significant degree of crisis intervention (or psychotherapy) when not working in disasters, will often be amazed by some of the seriously important information that gets revealed right at the end of a session, when someone realizes an interview is drawing to a close.

It is also a good idea to keep the possibility of abusive behavior in mind. Physical or psychological child abuse, spouse abuse, elder abuse, or other abusive relationships may all be uncovered by a DMH worker during routine screening interviews. If individuals had trouble controlling their tempers prior to the disaster, their conditions will likely remain the same, or worsen, after being subjected to greater levels of stress during the recovery period.

HELP AND SEEK-HELP BEHAVIORS

Farberow (1978a, pp. 9-12; 1978d, pp. 18-19) offered this list of behavioral clues that he termed "Help and Seek-Help Behaviors." Readers interested in having yet another framework for screening individuals suspected of having serious difficulties may find this to be a more practical approach (see Table 1, pp 90-91). Criteria such as these, and most other information published by CMHS, are considered to be in the public domain, and it is their authors' hope that it will be reprinted and cited so that more people can become aware of techniques and issues such as these. This free access makes it especially easy to design reproducible DMH training material and handouts.

TABLE 1: HELP AND SEEK-HELP BEHAVIORS*

Alertness and Awareness

+ You can probably handle the situation if the client:

1. Is aware of who he [she] is, where he [she] is, and what has happened;
2. Is only slightly confused or dazed, or shows slight difficulty in thinking clearly or concentrating on a subject.

- Consider referral to a mental health agency if the client:

1. Is unable to give own name or names of people with whom he [she] is living;
2. Cannot give date, state where he [she] is, or tell what he [she] does;
3. Cannot recall events of past 24 hours;
4. Complains of memory gaps.

Actions

+ You can handle if the client:

1. Wrings his [her] hands, appears stiff and rigid, clenches his [her] fists;
2. Is restless, mildly agitated, and excited;
3. Has sleep difficulty;
4. Has rapid or halting speech.

- Consider referral if the client:

1. Shows agitation, restlessness, pacing;
2. Is apathetic, immobile, unable to arouse self to movement;
3. Is incontinent;
4. Mutilates self;
5. Excessively uses alcohol or drugs;
6. Is unable to care for self, for example, doesn't eat, drink, bathe, change clothes;
7. Repeats ritualistic acts.

*From Farberow, 1978a, pp. 9-12; 1978d, pp. 18-19.

Speech

+ You can handle if the client:

1. Has appropriate feelings of depression, despair, discouragement;
2. Has doubts about his [her] ability to recover;
3. Is overly concerned with small things, neglecting more pressing problems;
4. Denies problems; states he [she] can take care of everything himself [herself];
5. Blames his [her] problems on others; is vague in his [her] planning; is bitter in his [her] feeling of anger that he [she] is a victim.

- Consider referral if the client:

1. Hears voices, sees visions, or has unverified bodily sensations;
2. States his [her] body feels unreal and he [she] fears he [she] is losing his [her] mind;
3. Is excessively preoccupied with one idea or thought;
4. Has the delusion that someone or something is out to get him [her] and his [her] family;
5. Is afraid he [she] will kill self or another;
6. Is unable to make simple decisions or carry out everyday functions;
7. Shows extreme pressure of speech; talk overflows.

Emotions

+ You can handle if the client:

1. Is crying, weeping, and continues retelling the disaster;
2. Has blunted emotions, little reaction to what is going on around him [her];
3. Shows excessive laughter, high spirits;
4. Is easily irritated and angered over trifles.

- Consider referral if the client:

1. Is excessively flat, unable to be aroused, or completely withdrawn;
2. Is excessively emotional, shows inappropriate emotional reactions.

SUICIDAL PERSON?
(QUESTIONS TO ASK)

My experience has been that very few disaster victims are so deeply depressed that they will present themselves as being at risk for suicide. Nevertheless, it is a possibility, and persons not accustomed to interviewing someone to assess that risk will probably appreciate these guiding questions:

1. **What has happened that makes life not worth living?** Do not try to solve the problem; just listen and help them clarify their thoughts. The more reasons given, the higher the risk.

2. **What are your reasons for wanting to live?** The fewer the reasons, the higher the risk.

3. **What are your reasons for wanting to die?** The more reasons, the higher the risk.

4. **How often do you think about suicide?** The more often, the higher the risk.

5. **How intensely do you feel like this? How do you behave when you feel this way?** Look for signs of isolation and serious intent.

6. **How long do these depressed/suicidal periods last?** The longer, the higher the risk.

7. **Have you ever attempted suicide? (If so, How?)** Even gestures are important, and the more serious the previous attempt, the higher the risk.

8. **How long ago was the (most recent) attempt?** The closer in time, the higher the risk.

9. **Has a family member or friend attempted or committed suicide?** Explore who, when, how, and why (plus how the person you are interviewing feels about the deceased). Children, for instance, will often talk about wanting to be with a deceased parent or grandparent. An elderly person who has lost a mate may make similar statements about joining that person.

10. **How would you do it? When? Where? and, Where will your (significant others) be?** Even a nonlethal means is cause for concern if the person believes it will

be fatal. Once the means has been established, eliminate it.

11. **On a scale of 1 to 10, what is the probability you will actually go through with it?** The higher the number, the higher the risk.

12. **Whom do you trust the most to help keep this from happening?** Find that person and make him or her a part of the plan that will protect this person. In fact, involve as many others as possible. Notify family, friends, clergy, and others in the person's support system and make appropriate referrals. Do this in the presence of the person you are trying to help so that he or she is aware of all the steps that have been taken.

If there is not imminent danger, make a written contract (Table 2, p. 94) with the person that he or she will call a crisis hotline or someone from the support system before taking any self-destructive actions. Have the person sign it with you (and with any others who are part of the support team), and each of you should keep a copy. Have people check on this person frequently for monitoring and support.

If there does appear to be imminent danger, take the necessary steps to have the person evaluated by others who will decide whether or not voluntary or involuntary hospitalization is needed. You may even need to petition for a mental health commitment, if you are the only one who has had contact with the person and the person refuses treatment. The commitment process provides a means by which the person at risk can be picked up, detained, evaluated, and, if necessary, treated against his or her will until the period of threat to self or others has ended.

If, in your own practice, you customarily use other methods to conduct brief assessments of depression, anxiety and panic episodes, thought and mood disorders, and/or suicidal risk, take whatever forms you need with you and use them as part of your DMH protocol. Commonly used, quick-scoring measures like the "Beck Depression Inventory" (Beck, 1978) can be very useful in the field.

TABLE 2: SAMPLE CONTRACT

_____

Date

I promise that I will not attempt to kill myself, or do anything that would cause me to be seriously injured between now and _____ (date of next appointment with his/her treatment professional). If I feel like I might be tempted to harm myself between now and then, I will call _____ (crisis hotline phone number) and I will alert _____ (significant others involved in his his/her treatment plan).

_____

Signature

_____

Witness (family member/friend)

_____

Witness (DMH worker)

PROBLEMS WITH
DISPLACED FEELINGS/EMOTIONS

Sometimes the combination of a stress response (especially an adrenalin rush) and the strong bonds that form in times of disaster can lead to confused feelings and emotions. People under severe stress may be inclined to misinterpret the events that are occurring around them. I have seen two examples of this recently.

In the first situation, a man who had lost his wife in a disaster became close to a woman who was helping him. Although forming tight bonds is common, he apparently mistook her kind and caring nature for the development of a romantic relationship, despite knowing she was happily married. This frightened both parties, angered the worker, and destroyed their relationship. Defusing the situation with the worker and explaining why I thought this had occurred seemed to provide her some measure of relief, but the relationship, as it had been, was over.

The other recent example came when I interviewed a first-time worker after she returned home. This married woman reported, with some amazement, that male relief workers were constantly "hitting on her" (trying to get her to be romantically and/or sexually involved with them) during her tour of duty. While some might conclude these guys might have just been "horny jerks" (men who had poor social skills and appeared interested in having a casual sexual relationship with her), I suspect that their behavior had to do with the same dynamic I noted previously. People in disasters are under a lot of stress, and helpers reach out to them as an act of kindness and support. The reassuring comments and helping gestures made by DMH workers (and other helpers) are sometimes misinterpreted as romantic interest or sexual attraction.

Although these two examples have involved cases of mistaken love interests, the effects can just as easily involve confused and displaced feelings of anger and hate. Someone who has just had a bad time with his or her insurance carrier may discharge an emotional blast at a relief worker for no reason that is readily apparent to the poor, unsuspecting worker. Afterwards, both will feel terrible and neither will likely know what it was all about. Workers need to remain alert to these phenomena and try to constantly monitor how their actions are being perceived by those victims and workers with whom they are in close contact.

By the way, if I am wrong and the relief workers mentioned before do turn out to be "horny jerks," they should be singled out and called to the attention of supervisory personnel. In an ARC operation, they probably would be sent home. Sexual harassment, or any sexually inappropriate behavior, is neither wanted nor tolerated on the job.

Chapter 9

OTHER ASPECTS OF DISASTER MENTAL HEALTH

Now that some of the fundamental elements of one-to-one DMH work with victims and workers have been explored, it is time to move ahead into some of the broader aspects of the work. This section will examine documentation, triage, serving as the on-call worker, the DMH role at headquarters, handling stressors in the work environment, and several more tricks of the trade (practical practice issues).

DOCUMENTATION

Required DMH documentation will vary from job to job and from organization to organization, so I will again draw from my ARC experiences. There are generally five types of written material that may be needed: casenotes, referrals, purchase orders (or other forms for authorization of purchased goods and services), statistics, and narratives. If you cannot function without a skillful secretary or an adept administrative assistant, you are probably in for a shock, because paperwork is generally the responsibility of each worker.

CASENOTES

Casenotes are written for any of the more serious interventions that are made. This will include victim or worker situations, when formal treatment is arranged, when referrals to other agencies are made, when services are authorized for payment, or when some other special handling has taken place (e.g., a worker has been relieved of duty and sent home). ARC has a special form that is used for DMH casenotes. The forms are then kept confidential and are not filed in any readily accessible location. Believe it or not, only a very small number of cases need any written notes. Most DMH contacts are brief, self-contained interventions that require no formal notes—just a few hash marks on a statistical tally sheet.

REFERRALS

Referrals often come to ARC DMH staff, in writing (on a special form called a 1475), from staff in other ARC specializations. DMH workers will acknowledge the referral by noting something like "client received" on the same form. With that limited feedback, the referring worker knows the person was seen, and the person's chart will reflect the contact, but confidentiality is maintained.

Outgoing referrals require a signed release form and can be done verbally or in writing. When making referrals for ongoing treatment, be sensitive to the victims' financial status and insurance coverage. Many people now have managed care health insurance policies with written restrictions about whom they can see for mental health services, if they expect to use their coverage. Health maintenance organization (HMOs) plans and employee assistance programs (EAPs), for instance, will limit the programs to which you can refer their people, they may require precertification, and the covered individuals may have to first speak with or see their primary-care physician (or provider group). As someone who works in a public sector mental health center, I have seen how angry people can become when they find out their coverage will not reimburse them for services they received from our agency.

Be sensitive to the victims' more personal desires and needs. Some may prefer working with a program affiliated with their religious beliefs (such as Lutheran Services or Catholic Social Agency), or may prefer seeing someone in private practice or going to a nonprofit agency, rather than a public, government-funded agency. The better you target your referrals, the more likely the people are to follow through and receive the needed services with a minimum number of difficulties.

WRITTEN AUTHORIZATIONS

Written authorizations to purchase mental health-related items or services can be issued by ARC DMH workers. Examples of such purchases are compassionate items (a stuffed toy for a child who has suffered a major loss) or a few therapy sessions from a local provider (if the victim has no other funding available for the services). As noted earlier, ARC refers to these authorizations as disbursing orders (DOs). Because they are as good as cash, they must be properly used and carefully safeguarded.

STATISTICS

Statistics compiled by ARC DMH workers are kept on a simple, single-page form. Whenever a significant contact has occurred, workers place a hash mark in the appropriate spot to indicate if it was an adult or child contact, a victim or a worker, a counseling session or a defusing/debriefing, and so on. There are also spots to note if a home visit was done, or if other community contacts were made. Workers do a daily total of the numbers for each category and phone them into headquarters. These figures, once combined with everyone else's statistics, help determine future expenses and staffing needs.

NARRATIVES

Narratives are sought from most ARC workers at the end of their assignments. The narratives often include background information, a summary of duties performed by the writer, a description of any relationship issues (e.g., How well did DMH workers and representatives of other functions work together?), the worker's final job statistics, and comments on what worked well and what still needs work (in order to be more effective next time). Narratives are very important for analyzing the job and planning for future disasters.

Supervisory level workers will have a great deal of additional documentation to worry about. They will be maintaining staff rosters, writing performance evaluations, handling various logistical documents, communicating with other relief functions, maintaining and distributing relevant educational and referral materials, helping generate press releases, possibly doing recruitment, and so on. More laptop computers are showing up in supervisors' luggage as they are getting their paperwork organized and saving whatever portions of it they can for use on future assignments. More information for supervisors will be offered in a later chapter.

TRIAGE

The process of screening a large group of victims (or workers) who are all potential DMH clients, and then setting priorities among them based upon their level of need, is called *triage*. To an individual DMH worker thrust on the front lines, triage often becomes a simple matter of doing one of two things:

1. seeing whoever is referred (or appears) on a first-come, first-served basis, or
2. seeing whoever screams the loudest (either literally or figuratively).

As workers from other functions get to know you, they will begin pushing you to be sure you see their clients as soon as possible. As victims get to know you, they will also refer more people. Before you know it, you will be quite busy doing lots of what Myers (1994) refers to as *microlevel* intervention.

The problem with this is that, if DMH workers handle the mental health needs of their catchment area only through one-to-one interventions, the psychological needs of the broader community might easily be overlooked. Ideally, some time needs to be spent on *macrolevel* intervention—consultation, education, and outreach to schools, residential care institutions, community agencies, government officials, and the media, so that information gets out to the many other persons in need who otherwise may never come to the attention of any relief organization (Myers, 1994).

To supervisors, triage involves maintaining greater emphasis on taking a macro perspective to relief efforts. More of their duties must center on consultation activities with key individuals and groups operating in the disaster area. A major portion of their managerial role is to find the areas of the population with the greatest need for DMH intervention and target limited resources accordingly.

ON-CALL SERVICES

In any large operation, DMH workers will need to establish 24-hour coverage for mental health emergencies that may arise among the other workers or among the persons being housed in shelters. DMH people can generally share this duty on a rotating basis if there are several DMH workers being housed close to one another. In ARC operations, there will always be on-call health workers as well. They tend to be quite a bit busier.

DMH calls can arise in cases where someone is decompensating, for whatever reason. A worker might receive bad news from home and need immediate counseling and support. A sheltered victim might break down under the stress of recent events. News of expected bad weather might have everyone on edge.

Try to be sure that you are housed with most of the other workers, as that makes for fast and easy emergency access. Beepers and cellular phones are usually scarce and, when available, are prone to malfunctioning. Keep key contact people alerted to your whereabouts. My experience has been that DMH on-call people are seldom called, but the security that is offered by having someone assigned is important in and of itself.

THE DISASTER MENTAL HEALTH ROLE AT HEADQUARTERS

DMH workers are often needed to assist DMH supervisory staff with several of the functions that are carried out in a field headquarters. Tasks there may include:

1. welcoming and orienting new DMH staff (and staff from other specialties) to prepare them for both their job duties and the stresses they may encounter.
2. defusing and debriefing staff members, as problems arise or as they leave at the end of their tours of duty.
3. mediating staff disputes.
4. helping gather and record statistics about DMH interventions.
5. maintaining an inventory of DMH brochures, training material, and supplies.
6. advising the media about DMH concerns.

7. developing a list of referral resources (or keeping it current).
8. consulting with representatives of other agencies that may be a part of providing mental health services in the area.
9. keeping track of the workers who are arriving and leaving, to help assure adequate coverage.
10. helping with recruitment, if there are not enough workers to meet the needs.
11. attending community meetings where a DMH presence may be worthwhile.
12. assisting with day-to-day supervision and support of other DMH staff members (or staff from other functions) who are working out in the service centers, shelters, meal centers, and so on.

Yes, there is a lot of paperwork, just as in any other large administrative undertaking. Some workers have told me that they were bored working at headquarters and would have preferred a full-time field assignment. This seems to be particularly true for first-time workers.

During my second ARC disaster assignment, I served in this role and found it to be a very positive experience. I think it was successful because I did get to be involved with many of the activities listed previously and I got to do a lot of outreach to DMH workers in the field. More information about this will be covered in the upcoming chapter on supervisory issues.

THE WORK ENVIRONMENT

Spend as much time as possible before, during, and after the work day mingling with workers from all of the different specializations. This contact yields a wealth of information about the working conditions everyone is facing, both individually and collectively. Part of the DMH role is to seek out information about negatively stressful working conditions and advocate for change.

The mental health of an entire group of workers can be adversely influenced by environmental factors such as:

poor lighting
understaffing
malfunctioning equipment
high noise levels
lack of breaks/time off
overcrowding
extremes in temperature/humidity
supply shortages
absence of items needed for comfort and/or recreation
unavailability of (or poor choices in) snack foods, drinks, and/or meals

When problems are discovered, communicate them to the staff members who have clout. Members of the health services staff, the supervisors in DMH (and other specialties), and/or the center or shelter managers, probably can orchestrate corrective action.

Arrangement of furniture and the strategic placement of a snack/drink area near the entrance to a shelter or service center can do much to help put newcomers at ease. Offering food or drink to those waiting in line makes a fine icebreaking activity for DMH workers seeking to make contact with people entering the facility. The canteen area is also a spot where DMH workers can make important contacts with other staff members to monitor stress levels, behavior, and emotional needs.

Inappropriate conduct by one or more workers can easily cause major disruptions in an otherwise calm work environment. DMH workers need to be alert to workers displaying behavior indicative of:

racism
sexism
ageism
any other overt prejudices
sexual harassment
constant complaining and/or negativistic attitudes
open hostility and/or overt expressions of anger
substance abuse problems
any warning signs of serious mental illness

These kinds of misbehavior can seriously undermine the morale of an entire group of people and can even cause good workers to want to leave the operation prematurely. It is best to try to recognize and resolve problems quickly. If they cannot be corrected, have the offending workers removed and sent home.

Where victims' or staff members' behavior is potentially disruptive, either to the work environment or to a living environment (as might be the case in a shelter), it is often best to attempt to isolate the problematic individuals. Try to make special arrangements to see them (or house them) somewhere apart from the rest of the group. The same types of individuals who present therapeutic challenges in our day-to-day careers (e.g., persons with traits indicative of any serious personality disorder) can easily be present within disaster operations. DMH workers need to carefully watch over the needs of these troubled individuals while, at the same time, monitoring the whole group's psychological well-being.

Occasionally, relief organizations are faced with fraudulent opportunists who were not in the area at the time when the disaster occurred — people who came to the area to try to obtain money for housing and/or replacement items for which they are not entitled. In ARC, routine interviews by trained family service workers generally screen out most of the people making fraudulent claims.

Once deceptive individuals have been denied whatever they were seeking, some people will become angry, loud, and demanding, and their behavior will quickly require DMH intervention. In addition to my use of crisis intervention skills, I have found that the timely disbursement of a small amount of snack food and drinks can help resolve the situation, as you will see in the following example.

A young, homeless man with a history of physical and mental illness was drifting through a disaster area several weeks after the damaging storm which prompted the relief effort. Under questioning, his ever-changing stories clearly indicated he had not been in the area at the time when the disaster struck. When confronted, he eventually admitted having been several hours away on the day in question. When told he could not get the money and services he was seeking through ARC, he began crying and making a scene in the service center.

I took him aside, we talked, and I allowed him as much food and drink from our canteen as he wished while we talked about his history, problems, and needs. He had not eaten in several days prior to entering our service center. As he ate his fill of our snacks, he was calming down and I had managed to buy the time I needed to allow our staff to contact a local homeless shelter and refer him for the needed help which we could not offer him. We sent him on his way with a small bag of additional juice and snacks, having managed to avert a potentially nasty scene in our facility.

The very nature of a work setting, and/or its location within a community, can become a major stressor for some individuals. Following the Los Angeles earthquake, for example, shelters were needed. Given the history of problems with urban violence and gang activity in some of the neighborhoods, and the mix of residents in the shelters, there was some increased potential for problems that ordinarily do not exist in most sheltering situations. Residents and staff members may need extra support in coping with these kinds of tense situations. Uniformed security guards or police officers are sometimes useful in these situations. Their presence can provide a sense of both physical and psychological security to the persons working or living in these settings.

Paying careful attention to personal safety is a good idea at all times, but it is especially important when you are operating in a foreign environment. Sadly, there are occasions when relief volunteers and staff members become victims of crimes while on assignment. As is so often the case with tourists in an unfamiliar city, there are those who will go after strangers as their targets for criminal behavior. Anyone who is victimized will need special attention from their coworkers, supervisors, and DMH workers.

In some work locations there may be environmental hazards of other types. Insects (e.g., mosquitos and fire ants), snakes, alligators, other animals that may have been displaced by the disaster, poisonous plants (e.g., poison ivy and poison oak), the strong, burning rays of the sun, communicable diseases, heat, and other dangers may be present. ARC and most other relief organizations offer briefings about such conditions when newcomers enter an operation. Exercising proper hygiene practices and taking appropriate personal safety precautions with these matters can spare you from nasty complications during your assignment.

Although the discussion thus far has highlighted several negative aspects of the disaster relief environment, there are often positive features to consider. Workers in disasters tend to get caught up in the fast pace of relief work, and victims become wrapped up in their own recovery efforts. Both groups tend to overlook the splendor in nature that surrounds them. Disasters rarely are so catastrophic that they destroy everything in an area. Take time out to enjoy the beauty that lingers and help victims to do the same. It is easy for people to forget the reasons they may have chosen to settle there in the first place. Their houses may be gone, but the land and its charm will remain.

MORE TRICKS OF THE TRADE

The more familiarity a DMH worker has with CI and outreach, the easier many assignments will be. Generally speaking, whatever skills and techniques you have learned to use in your regular practice will serve you well in DMH assignments. In the event you still feel the need for more *"How to ..."* information, and maybe even a few gimmicks, here are some additional ways to help assure a positive DMH experience.

1. **Cultivate Understanding and Support from Clients, Colleagues, and Employers Before Going Out on Assignment.** The ability to drop everything on short notice and run to a disaster site is not something everyone can easily achieve. I have found that my private clients seem to have the least problem with my occasional jaunts. I prepare them in advance for the possibility that it may happen and then, if it does, they never seem to mind (and, in fact, many seem pleased that I volunteer my services in this way).

   Colleagues are generally not a problem either, unless they will end up doing your work while you are away. Even then, most people will be supportive, whether or not there is a chance that they may have to cover your cases during the time that you are off on assignment.

Employers tend to be the snags. Taking vacation time works, but this leaves little time for your real vacations. The goal is to try to arrange for some or all of your time at the disaster to be paid administrative leave time, similar to jury duty or military reserve time. Some employers will grant this up to a preset number of days per year. It helps to tell them what you are interested in doing well in advance and see if they can support it with paid time. If the disaster is close by, and you have already laid a foundation with your employer by establishing ties with your professional organization and with ARC (or another VOAD group), then some amount of administrative time is generally very easy to obtain. In fact, in some situations in which help has been requested and other agencies are sending employees, releasing you will be the politically correct thing for your employer to do. My employer allows me up to 10 days per year.

Because I used to teach college and graduate courses on a part-time basis, I occasionally had to arrange a substitute teacher for a class. For one job, the ARC disaster relief coordinator in my area's local chapter was kind enough to volunteer her time and substitute for me one evening. It helped that she had her doctorate in a related field. I have also substituted for a friend of mine who needed to miss his class while he was out at his first major disaster. Part of your own readiness planning needs to include working with your employers to develop the flexibility you need to be able to go out on assignments.

2. **Take Your Training Manual(s) and Favorite DMH Handouts With You When You are Sent Out to a Disaster Area**. It is very important to have your key DMH books and training materials with you for easy reference at all times. It is also helpful to carry a few pamphlets, handouts, and sample press releases on stress management, children's behavior in disasters, and so on, especially if you are among the first persons dispatched to the area. Pick some up from your local ARC office and learn to keep a copy of everything you get that is new and looks helpful. Take this book, too.

3. **Carry Your Most Needed DMH Supplies With You to the Job.** Most large job sites will have some toys, therapeutic coloring books (about floods, hurricanes, etc.), and art supplies, but small or newly established sites may not have these things. If you cannot work with children without crayons, markers, certain toys or games, and so on, take some with you. Then you can quickly get started seeing people, rather than worrying about ordering supplies.

4. **Wear a Picture ID and Introduce Yourself to Everyone.** Having the ID (and accessories such as a shirt, hat, or jacket with a logo) helps reassure people that you officially belong there. That simple step makes it easier for you to generate contacts and build trust. As time goes by, people will seek you out.

5. **Share Information About Your Personal Style.** When you are getting to know your coworkers, it is a good idea to let them know something about your personality and your preferred intervention style. For instance, I like to first take some time and observe potential problems in interviews between others. I will intervene only if I am invited to do so, unless things really appear to be getting out of hand. If the other staff expect you to jump in and assist them at the first sign that any sad or angry emotions are being expressed by a survivor or a fellow worker, and you do not do so, they may conclude you are not very observant and/or you are not doing your job.

On my first assignment I had not alerted others to my style. One day an angry woman came into the service center and began challenging her family service caseworker. She was complaining he had not done enough for her, venting a lot of anger at him that had sprung from her material losses; she seemed to be trying to evoke an angry response from him. Although he had no formal training in counseling (he was a businessman by profession), he remained calm, let her vent, calmed her down, and managed to even get her to realize the dynamics of her angry rantings.

This difficult interview went on for some time. Others kept glancing at me and nonverbally indicating that I needed to go over and save this poor guy. My sense, on the other hand, was that he was doing fine, and any effort to poke my nose into this woman's affairs would have only upset her further and prolonged the ordeal for all of us.

Afterwards I spoke to the man and praised his skills. He had done a fine job in a very difficult circumstance, and he had done it with his own natural helping skills. He was pleased to hear from me that no one could have done it any better than he had done. Once he and the others realized why I handled the situation in the way I did, everyone accepted my actions in the situation. In retrospect, I have found that it works better to alert others that this will be my preferred approach to similar occurences.

6. **Take Out the Garbage, Vacuum, and Make Coffee.** Not too many people will fight with you over helping with these chores (or any similar ones) while you are in your work site. What will happen as a result of doing some chores is that other workers will be so pleased to see you pitching in and helping in these ways that it will enhance your image. It shows others that you consider yourself to be a regular person, no better than anyone else on the job. It will also result in making workers from other specialties feel more comfortable about seeking you out and talking to you if the time comes that they feel they need your help.

7. **Work the Crowds.** There are often many people waiting in lines (for services or for food), living in shelters, or working a clean up. By spending a few minutes with lots of people at one time, larger numbers of people can be screened and given a bit of support. Once individuals realize your role and get to know (and trust) you, they will give you referrals on friends and family members who are also in need of help.

Talking to a crowd is also a much easier way to begin with a wary audience than singling someone out. Have you ever had the experience of staffing an information booth at a health fair? No one wants to be the only one seen publicly talking to a counselor, even if the subject is stress management. But if there are two or three people there talking to the staff, other people will generally walk up and begin speaking more freely. Victims find that there is definitely safety in numbers.

8. **Make Condolence Visits to Families Who Have Lost Loved Ones.** They, perhaps more than any other victims, need to tell their stories about the disaster and feel the support of their community. Although not everyone will allow you to talk to them, most survivors will welcome your visit and relish the time you spend with them. Some of my most rewarding DMH moments have occurred during condolence calls.

    If there are many casualties and you are involved early enough to do so, consider working right at the morgue. People will need assistance as they come in to identify the bodies of their loved ones. This is tough duty. Work with a partner or arrange to meet someone afterwards to aid you in defusing your own feelings. See Appendix B (p. 175-183) for a case example of work at a large morgue operation.

9. **Visit the Remote Work Sites to Assess and Address the Needs of the Staff Members Working There.** Large relief operations have warehouses, mass-care kitchens, and other logistical staging areas staffed with people who might accidentally be overlooked. Go visit them and help unload a truck, cook or serve a meal, and so on. There is no better way to get to know the people there than by pitching in and helping them do their jobs.

10. **Learn About and Visit the Usual Community Gathering Places.** Every town has places where people congregate — a square, the schools and churches, drop-in-centers, town hall, the fire station, diners, and so on. You can take the pulse of the community by spending time at places like these. In one tornado-ravaged city that I visited, I searched for quite a while, feeling more like a private detective than a DMH worker, before being able to do a condolence call with a man who had lost his wife and daughter in the storm. That visit took

place under a huge tree, in a small park behind a gas station, when I finally found that town's community gathering place.

11. **Find and Use the Community's Natural Helpers.** Every place I have worked has had a wealth of people who were not formally trained as helpers but, for one reason or another, grew into their helping roles. In one small Florida town that had been hit by a tidal flood, it was the local postmaster and the librarian. These two women were seeing lots of people, most of whom they knew quite well, come and go from their work places. Each day they would clue me in on who needed a visit. They could usually even tell me how those from the previous days' visits were doing. Before our ARC team left their town, I provided them (and a few other natural helpers) with a mini-workshop and with several handouts on emotional first aid, stress management, and other aspects of the recovery process, to help them continue the fine work they were doing.

Myers (1994) notes that there will be occasions when cultural, ethnic, or language barriers, or other privacy concerns of a community, will preclude the effective use of DMH outsiders. Indigenous workers can be used, if they are available in sufficient numbers and if they are not already overwhelmed by their own matters of recovery. In those instances when enough trained workers simply are not available, it is often necessary to train and use the natural helpers who volunteer their services as caregivers.

12. **Develop Support Groups for Victims.** This can be easily done by working with local agencies, churches, or schools. Find a suitable location that is close to most victims' residences and obtain permission to use a meeting room. Select a time for a weekly meeting that will not interfere with most work schedules. Get someone who has computer skills or artistic talent to make up a flyer that can circulate as a poster or handout. Foster a relationship with a community person who can facilitate after you have gone home. Get public service coverage about it in newspapers and on radio and televi-

sion, and have other relief workers spread the word. Then go for it! If that seems like too much work, just visit existing support group meetings, take their emotional pulse, do a one-shot debriefing, and offer handouts.

13. **Use a Buddy-System Approach for Outreach Visits Whenever Possible.** When doing home visits or making outreach interventions with groups of people, it is often helpful to travel with a partner. This benefits you in several ways—by allowing two people to be interviewed at once, offering different points of view on tough cases, and providing a vehicle for mutual support. Unfortunately, staffing patterns will generally make this difficult to do, because there are seldom enough DMH workers as it is. There are, however, several good alternatives.

    One idea is to team up with people from other specializations. For instance, you might take a nurse or an emergency medical technician (EMT) if there are also physical health issues to be addressed. Another idea is to go out with a local volunteer. This can really be helpful in keeping you from getting lost and in briefing you about local culture and customs. A third option is to save the tough stuff for a day when a supervisor or another DMH worker is going to be in the area and can accompany you.

14. **Keep in Close Touch With the Rest of the Relief Team**. Whenever you go out to do outreach visits, either by yourself or with a partner, be sure to inform others about where you will be working and when you think you will return. You should also call in or stop back to your base of operations as often as possible, especially if you are the only DMH worker in that setting. The other workers need to know that you are available to them, especially if something comes up that requires your attention. This will also better provide for your own safety, security, and support needs.

15. **Stress Testing Cards Are a Great Way to Break the Ice**. Some time ago, at an NASW annual meeting, a vendor in the exhibit area gave me a stress card. These cards

are like the old mood rings; when you hold them with your thumb for a few seconds, they change colors to indicate your stress level (skin temperature). I took mine along on my first ARC DMH trip and found it was a great way to get conversations started when approaching strangers in the waiting line. People see others try it and they immediately want to play with it, too.

One older gentleman and his middle-aged son each tried it one day. The son produced a perfect blue (the most calm reading it could be), while the dad could not move it off black (stressed out). The son told me (in front of his dad) that the dad had always been stressed out and would never change the color. Well, a day or two later, I saw the dad at the center, but the son was not along. He asked to try it again and, when he did, he produced the perfect shade of blue. He was really excited, but worried the son would not believe him. I took great pleasure in getting out a piece of official letterhead and writing a note to the son, certifying the calm blue state had, indeed, been achieved by his dad. If you have a card, or can get one, take it along.

16. **If You Are On-Call, Prepare a Ready-To-Go Bag.** Assemble your handouts, stress card, ID, manuals, business cards, a copy of your professional license, your driver's license, supplies, ARC chapter pins and job shirts, first-aid kit, flashlight, pocket knife, bug spray, sun block, insurance and prescription plan cards, medications (prescription and over-the-counter), money and/or travelers' checks, fanny pack (mini-suitcase worn as a belt), and so on, together in advance (or at least make a list that you can use as a check-off memory aid).

Also remember to pack any items you need to help you manage your own stress, such as a book, a radio or tape player (and spare batteries), jogging shoes, a video game, a bathing suit, and so on. Think back to your days in Scouting or the military, when you were taught to be prepared. You will have too many last-minute things to worry about as it is, and doing this little bit of preparation will lessen some of the stress on you.

17. **Pack Wisely and Travel With Light Bags**. This must seem like a really absurd comment after the previous list of several items you may want to take along (besides clothing and toiletries). The fact is, conditions at disaster sites are often less than ideal, and you may have to go to many places where bellmen and sky caps will not be available. Try not to take anything you cannot carry yourself, if things get rough. If you are going on a Red Cross job, ARC will help guide you in what to pack for the conditions where you will be going.

   Once you are there, you will probably accumulate even more baggage as you purchase and/or gather various souvenirs for yourself and for family members and friends. Some people travel with an empty, collapsible suitcase to be used for the trip home. Others will pack a box and ship it home via a parcel delivery service. Packing is one more thing to worry about for those of you who live by the motto, "When the going gets tough, the tough go shopping."

18. **Treat Everyone You Meet as if He or She Is Your Boss**. I originally conceived of this as, "treat folks like customers who are always right," but saying that, or giving any sort of Golden Rule admonition, does not go quite far enough. The nature of supervision in disasters is such that you may have very limited contact with your actual DMH supervisor. He or she may have to rely heavily upon information from others to do your evaluation.

   With this in mind, go out of your way to assure positive interactions with all victims and all other staff members. Keep supervisors from other specialties and/or the center and shelter managers apprised of your whereabouts and activities. Their impressions of you may help shape your disaster relief career.

19. **What About Cameras and Taking Pictures?** Photography is a hobby for me. I have carried my wife's small automatic 35mm camera along on all of my assignments, and I have managed to get some great damage-assessment-type shots for use in public speaking and training. Although I have not had any problems, others

with whom I have spoken did. Victims react negatively to feeling they are on display for tourists who have come to just gawk at them. Be careful to protect the dignity and privacy of the victims. This can easily be done by avoiding shooting any photos that include people. Whenever possible, explain why you are taking the photos and ask permission of home-owners before shooting anything on their property.

On my first job, I was working with a family whose home had been hit squarely in the middle by a tree, which had been tossed there by a tornado. The tree went through their roof and was still there when I saw them. It had just missed killing the father in his bed on the night of the storm. Because he had badly cut his hand while trying to remove it (and some large pieces of his tin roof that it had destroyed), the family was learning to live with it until he was well enough to continue the clean up. Their one-story home now had a huge hole in the center of its roof, with an open view (but for the tree) of the night sky.

After interviewing them, I asked to take a few pictures and they said that would be great. In fact, they did not have a camera and asked me to get a shot of it for them, with the father (whom I dubbed "the luckiest man in Florida") standing on the tree, on the roof, just above where he was almost killed. I got the film developed and stopped back with their prints before I left for home. They loved the photo and it appeared to be helping them resolve the events of their disaster.

20. **Do Not Forget the Folks Back Home**. No, this is not simply a reminder to call your mom (or mate or kids) occasionally during assignments, although that is very important too. This is, instead, a reminder to remember to watch out for the needs of everyone who is back home holding the fort while you are out on the road. Besides family and friends, there probably are others you might accidentally overlook. Many people are behind the scenes, doing the kinds of background work that keeps the organization going and makes your trip possible.

As an example, think about the people in ARC (or any other sponsoring organization) who are back in the local chapter office. They are fielding phone calls, gathering donations, and training additional recruits. My local ARC chapter trained 138 people during marathon sessions held around the time I was out on assignment for the 1993 Mississippi/Midwest floods. The pace is rapid, in part because many of those who usually help with this work have probably been sent out to the disaster. Those left behind are probably wishing they could be out in the field, too. All of this is creating lots of stress, and you may need to debrief the people you left behind, once you get back home.

The same is true for your family, friends, and coworkers. They carried the ball while you did your field service, and they experienced stressors just as you did. They may be building feelings of resentment toward you due to your absences. Be prepared to hear about their concerns. You will need to work at making a smooth reintegration from the role of DMH worker to the everyday roles you play in their world.

21. **Take a Day Off When You Return Home from an Assignment.** I know this is often hard to do, especially if you have already used lots of vacation time to go out on the assignment, but it is good to have a break between the relief work and the return to your regular duties, even if it means having to cut your trip 1 day short. You will be very tired; try to rest and reflect upon the experience. An upcoming section will deal more fully with the many issues associated with returning home from an assignment.

Chapter 10

LOSS, BEREAVEMENT, AND GRIEVING

Crises involving grief will usually send people into a long period of emotional turmoil. The resolution process often requires major reorganization of many aspects of one's life, because of unexpected changes in family units and/or support networks. Several factors may influence the survivors' recovery, including how sudden and/or violent the loss, the age of the victim(s), cultural differences/patterns of mourning, and individuals' prior ability to cope with this level of stress.

Losses can be categorized in two basic types:

1. *Physical (tangible) losses* include deaths, destruction of a home, having property stolen, or losing a limb.
2. *Psychosocial (intangible) losses* include the breakup of relationships, the feelings of violation caused by a violent crime, or losses of qualities such as self-esteem, identity, or status.

Bereavement, the state of having suffered a loss, will often result in several changes in behavior that will, for the most part, fall into easily observable patterns:

1. *Normal Grief*—which, at times, may involve weeping, anger, guilt, disorientation, and lower overall levels of psychological functioning.
2. *Anticipatory Grief*—similar to normal grief and considered to be normal, with the difference being that it begins before the loss actually occurs (as often happens with a person battling a terminal illness). This is very common in weather-related disasters that have been predicted in advance (e.g., people living in an evacuation zone, as a hurricane or flood draws near).

3. *Delayed/Inhibited Grief*—when the normal grieving process is prevented or obstructed, or when it does not occur at the time of the loss, it often is not resolved and professional help becomes necessary. This is common when such things as bureaucratic red tape, construction delays, and/or litigation drag out the length of the disaster event.

4. *Chronic/Perpetual Grief*—an unresolved state resulting when a person responds to a loss by becoming emotionally frozen by the notion that he or she cannot go on (survive) without the missing person or element of his or her life; again, professional help is needed.

STAGES OF GRIEF REACTIONS

Grief will often begin with a period of emotional numbness, followed by periods of disorganization and despair. As time passes, reorganization begins to occur. Kubler-Ross (1969) proposes the following stages which individuals who are dying, as well as survivors, often pass through while learning to accept a loss:

1. *Denial*—unconscious refusal to accept the loss.
2. *Bargaining*—attempting to "make a deal" with God, in order to avert the reality of the situation.
3. *Anger*—rather globally directed at things other than the real issue at hand.
4. *Depression*—as the anger turns inward, typical signs of depression such as loss of appetite, withdrawal, crying spells, loss of interest in routine activities, and so on, begin to appear.
5. *Acceptance*—the calm at the end of the storm of emotions which have occurred to this point.

People frequently seem to move in and out of the grieving state. These stages are not experienced by everyone, the stages may not occur in this order, and they may even overlap one another. Nevertheless, being familiar with these stages tends to be of practical use in helping gauge progress (and educate survivors).

Weiss (1987) reviewed current literature on the phases of grief and reported four phases of normal grieving that are different from those noted previously:

1. *Disbelief* — trouble accepting the reality of the loss (and the necessary changes that must now take place), possibly accompanied by denial that it even occurred.
2. *Protest* — a period of tearfulness, refusal to accept consolation, and yearning for the return of the lost individual.
3. *Despair* — a time when acceptance of the loss is just beginning, but persons continue to have feelings of hopelessness and helplessness when contemplating life without the lost person.
4. *Adaptation* — the point at which a new and separate identity and life plan become available.

He notes that individuals will progress through these at their own pace and may sometimes regress to an earlier stage.

FACTORS THAT MAY COMPLICATE BEREAVEMENT

Weiss (1987) goes on to note several factors that may lead to poor outcomes. He refers to the first one as *totally unexpected bereavement* — the sudden death of a loved one who was lost under conditions that were not at all expected to occur, as is the situation with most disaster-related deaths. This element of surprise and shock can be a confounding factor resulting in poor recovery. The reason may be as simple as the fact that this kind of death is so contrary to our expectations: healthy people are not supposed to die.

The second complicating factor he lists is *ambivalence about the lost relationship*. In couples who have high-conflict marriages/relationships, the survivor often reacts with mixed emotions to the loss of the mate. This often leads to problems with unresolved guilt, anger, and feelings of remorse. The same thing may occur with similarly troubled parent-child relationships.

The third and final factor he lists involves people who have been close emotionally, but have also had *relationships charac-*

terized by dependency, when one person is dependent upon the other for matters of routine functioning. If people do not drive, shop, or cook, for instance, they will have to make greater adjustments in their lives than they would have had to make if they had been more independent. Again this may be seen in couples or parent-child relationships following a death.

The disaster itself may even complicate bereavement, in cases where the loss occurred before the disaster event. If someone lost a mate (or other close friend or relative) shortly before the disaster, his or her mourning will be interrupted by recovery efforts.

I worked with an elderly gentleman who had lost his wife 2 months before the time when a flood damaged his home. He was already struggling to take over paying the bills and cooking, two of her former functions. Now he had to face a major new stressor, and all of the related clean up and paperwork, without his lifelong partner. I managed to get him hooked up with special aging support services, so that he would be less lonely, and with some volunteers from a clean up team, to help him tackle the mess.

TIMES NEEDING
SPECIAL ATTENTION

When family members and friends first arrive at the scene of a disaster and confront their losses, the harsh reality of the situation slaps them in the face. This is a critical point in time. People will display a variety of reactions and emotions. They may want and need a period of privacy, even from those who are there to help them.

Other stressful times for survivors are when they ask to see an injured person for the first time (or must identify a body), when they must notify other relatives and friends of their losses, when they must make funeral arrangements, and when they return to damaged homes and begin to salvage belongings.

Children who have suffered a loss will also need special attention, especially if it is the loss of someone who was very close to them and/or if the children have had no prior experience with death. Particularly troublesome for many adults will be the need to explain death to the children; answering their many questions about death; noting disaster losses and death-related themes that may begin to appear in their conversations, writings, art, and/or play (reenactments that are quite normal and generally helpful in processing the losses); possibly seeing some regressive behavior; and deciding whether to take children to memorial services and/or funerals.

Helpers need special attention upon completing interventions with survivors, particularly when doing grief counseling and/or condolence calls. These situations trigger all sorts of memories and emotions that should be shared and discussed before a worker begins his or her next interview. Seek out a coworker or a supervisor and spend a few minutes talking it out before moving on.

THERAPEUTIC TASKS
OF THE GRIEVING PROCESS

Osterweis and Townsend (1988a, 1988b) point out that the grieving process lasts much longer than most people realize. Although the worst is usually over by the end of 1 full year after a death, often it takes several years before feelings are fully resolved. Here are some of the key therapeutic tasks for DMH workers helping those who are grieving:

1. Help people confront the reality of the loss and begin to make the emotional separation that must occur before they can go on.
2. Guide the survivors' readjustment to the environment that is now dramatically changed by the lost person(s) and/or missing thing(s).
3. Facilitate survivors' reorganization of the other elements of their lives, so that they can form new connections with others and can make their lives whole again.
4. Educate people that grieving a major loss will normally be a long and difficult process; no one is expected to quickly feel better, or to be able to make all the necessary readjustments within any specific time frame. Teach them about anniversary reactions and about agencies and community support groups that will be able to provide support after you have gone. This is a form of stress inoculation that will pay off later.

5. Encourage individuals to use whatever support network is available to them. Bloom (1985), Osterweis and Townsend (1988a, 1988b), and many others have clearly found that social supports (such as visits from family, friends, clergy, and DMH workers) and support groups can play a major, positive role in influencing successful outcomes.

6. Help adults realize that children need to be involved in the grieving process, to whatever degree the children can understand and share in it. Children will sense the pain of the adults around them. Encourage adults to be open and honest with them about their own feelings and reactions. Whenever possible, adults must allow children to learn about (and be part of) the rituals that are a common aspect of death in our culture.

As is the case with any serious problems encountered during a DMH intervention, sometimes situations will require a referral for formal, ongoing treatment. Tecala (1993) operates the Center for Loss and Grief in Washington, DC, and she was one of the persons who provided CISD services to the emergency responders who served at the site of the 1983 Air Florida crash in Washington. She has identified several factors that suggest higher risk of developing PTSD because of the losses a victim has experienced:

1. Multiple deaths occurred.
2. Person was entombed or was injured without ability to get help (the longer the time, the higher the stress).
3. He or she is showing PTSD symptoms.
4. Multiple losses (physical and/or psychological).
5. Preexisting social problems/stressors.
6. Lack of social supports.
7. Premorbid mental health status.

Anyone with these risk factors will need careful screening and may well require more extensive therapeutic intervention than is possible via a brief DMH intervention.

Tecala (1993) reported success in treatment of severe cases of loss and PTSD using many of the same approaches listed earlier in this book. She also has many of her clients keep journals and she gives them assigned readings. She finds *bibliotherapy* (assigning readings) to be especially useful with shy persons who are unwilling to enter support groups or group therapy. Reading the thoughts, feelings, and reactions of others who faced similar tragedies helps them release, rather than repress, their emotions. There are also many books written for children that can help adults open a dialogue with them on the many issues of grief and loss.

Chapter 11

SELF-AWARENESS

To be optimally effective, DMH workers need to cultivate a sense of their own knowledge base, skills, capabilities, limitations, weaknesses, and needs. Self-awareness develops over time, as new situations are encountered. This section will discuss some issues that will help you begin to examine your own DMH character and image.

WHAT MOTIVATES DISASTER MENTAL HEALTH WORKERS?

The fact that DMH is exciting, and has addictive qualities, has already been mentioned, but just what is it that motivates a person to become involved as a helper in disaster relief programs? Are "crisis junkies" born that way (addicted to crisis stress), or are they created? What are the assets and liabilities of the personalities of relief workers? Unfortunately, I am not sure anyone fully understands the complex dynamics that are involved.

It is fairly easy to list qualities that many successful relief workers seem to have in common. Many of the best workers I have met share:

- altruism
- self-confidence
- a sense of humor
- belief in the goodness of others
- creativity
- a firm sense of family, community, and religious values
- compassion
- effective coping skills
- a need for adventure
- optimism

- a strong ability to carry out autonomous practice
- high energy levels
- a strong work ethic (and an equally strong play ethic, seen during their down time)
- flexibility
- professionalism and commitment to their careers
- friendly, outgoing natures
- a firm belief in the value of what they and their organizations are doing to help others

Relief workers who embody these qualities arrive at the job in a state of readiness for almost anything. They can find pleasure and support in their new environment, despite how outrageous the setting may be. They can give themselves positive strokes for the work they do, rather than expecting and seeking thanks from all of those they serve (or work alongside). They get things done, and they are a pleasure to be with, in the process.

Workers in whom these same qualities are limited (or nonexistent) tend to have more problems on the job. They will require more intensive supervision along all three supervisory dimensions (administration, education, and support). Their best shot at success might be to carve out a limited role for themselves which better matches their personality, skills, abilities, and personal needs. Usually, though, there just is not enough time to allow this kind of tailoring. These workers are more likely to leave the job early. They are less inclined to seek future assignments.

Bartone et al. (1989) have found that disaster workers who embody "dispositional resilience" (which they also dubbed "a personality style of hardiness") are more successful at fending off the usually negative effects of disaster stress. Many of the qualities and traits listed previously are consistent with hardiness and resilience.

Although altruism is probably the primary motivating factor for most disaster workers, there clearly are others. Kafrissen et al. (1975) note that some people will become involved "out of a sense of curiosity, not any real desire to help" (p. 162). Some may do it for the benefits volunteer affiliation affords them. Others probably do it to put meaningful activity in their lives. A few will try to use disaster work to meet personal needs in ways that are potentially more damaging. Farberow (1978d) cautions that there are those who do it out of a need to experience feelings of omnipotence or martyrdom. Others may use it as an escape from pressures at home.

I am a firm believer in the use of volunteer work as an adjunct therapy for persons with various types of mental illness. So much so, that an earlier work of mine (Weaver, 1993b) is designed solely to encourage it. In this case, though, I must voice a few words of caution. Although disaster work is very rewarding, it cannot be undertaken as a form of therapy or for filling glaring emotional needs in one's life. Those who attempt to use a disaster assignment in these inappropriate ways will generally find themselves painfully disappointed. The result may even include a lowering of someone's already weakened self-esteem.

SOURCES OF JOB STRESS

All workers bring a fair amount of emotional baggage along with them when they arrive at a disaster site. First, there is the normal stress associated with accepting a call to respond, tying up things at home, packing, and traveling. That is added to workers' preexisting levels of stress from routine concerns (family matters, employment issues, etc.).

Then there is the anticipatory stress relating to the disaster. Workers wonder:

- Where will I be working?
- What will I be seeing and doing?
- Will I be effective?

As each of us makes the switch from our predisaster responsibilities to those of DMH relief workers, we face the typical stresses associated with taking on a new job. Even veteran workers experience this stress, which is a natural part of making this substantial change in our lives.

Once on the job, Myers (1985) and others note there are more sources of stress, many of which are related to several areas of potential conflict for workers. These are some of the possibilities you may encounter, either directly or via defusing other workers:

1. **Worker and Victim Conflicts.** Disputes can arise over just about anything. It could be a specific disagreement over damage estimates or needed services, or the cause could be less clear. There can be tension from incompatible personalities, a clash of values, or insensitivity to issues of racial, ethnic, or cultural diversity.

2. **Worker and Coworker Conflicts.** These can occur within specialty functions (like DMH) or between different specialties. Squabbles can occur over anything ranging from a spat over a borrowed pen, chair, or vehicle, on up to a major disagreement about service provision to a shared victim, or a tiff over turf issues and each other's job responsibilities. Personalities, value systems, and issues of diversity can be factors here, too.

3. **Worker and Supervisor Conflicts.** These are very similar to worker and coworker conflicts but with the additional elements of power and control issues.

4. **Worker and Family Conflicts.** Even while away on assignment, workers can manage to get into disagreements by phone with relatives elsewhere. Or, workers' mates may be with them and be part of the job, allowing the opportunity for spats right in the work site.

5. **Personal Value Conflicts (Internal).** It does not always take two people to have a clash. Many workers struggle within themselves about issues brought to the surface by the disaster environment. First-time workers commonly grapple with issues brought on by the difference between expectation and reality. Many workers find themselves feeling caught between the infinite needs of the victims and the finite resources that are available for them to offer.

There are many other potential sources of stress on the job. There is always change of one sort or another. You will find yourself working and living in different cities, staying in unfamiliar types of housing, and driving cars other than those makes and models you are used to operating. Your boss is not usually someone with whom you are familiar, nor are you well acquainted with your new friends (and their little idiosyncrasies).

All of this may raise the odds of getting lost; having a traffic accident; developing sleep, appetite, and/or digestive problems; and so on.

Official misinformation can be yet another obstacle that many DMH workers will encounter all too frequently. Communication problems can easily occur between relief organizations and government officials/agencies, with the resultant confusion adding to everyone's stress level. Jacobs, Quevillon, and Stricherz (1990) note that the greatest potential for serious problems is in the identification of bodies and notification of family members of the deceased. The best practice is to be certain that critical information has been verified before you take any action (or further circulate it).

Here is one more thing to consider as you look toward future assignments: I have already mentioned problems with misplaced emotions, but Myers (1985) adds one more facet to that discussion. Citing the "strong sense of adventure and excitement" that most workers experience on the job, and the "seductiveness" of the work, she notes that a disaster "draws people to it and to each other . . . [hence] love affairs may occur" (p. 92). Be careful with relationships while working your disaster assignment; a failed romance is not something you will want to experience on top of the regular stresses of the job.

LIKING THE JOB TOO MUCH

Relief workers love to be out on assignment. Many who are not tied down by the responsibilities of caring for a family and/or holding a regular job are out for months at a time. They sometimes go from one job to the next without even a stop at whatever spot they call home. People love the work that much.

Unfortunately, having workers who are so strongly motivated to be out on assignment can sometimes lead to problems requiring the attention of health services and/or DMH workers. In their push to help, some workers will overlook their own physical and mental health problems and needs. Sometimes workers will arrive at the job in a state of poor health (or even full-blown illness), with conditions they probably failed to consider (or report) before leaving for the job. Individuals with high blood pressure are a common example. They may be doing fine in a low-stress environment at home, but, on the way to the job, their pressure skyrockets.

With any luck, routine health screening upon arrival at headquarters will catch many people with physical problems. The emotional problems, however, are often harder to catch. Those individuals may not show any outward signs of their conditions. In fact, their conditions may be under control, due to medications and/or environmental factors that are better controlled in their normal, home environments.

Depending upon the seriousness of their illnesses, some workers will be turned around and immediately sent home, without ever getting past the screening at headquarters. This is done for their own safety and well-being. Others who develop problems as they carry out their assignments may also need to be rested, treated, or possibly sent home.

Whatever the circumstances, and despite issues of personal safety, many will still hate to leave. They will need special attention and support to get them out the door and on the road to home. In cases where this occurs, it is often helpful to have the persons who are returning allow you to alert key individuals back home. It is good to let their support system know that they are coming, and that they may have special needs, because of the fact that they may have been unable to complete their assignments in the way they would have liked. When this happens in ARC, local chapters will help provide support upon a person's return home.

Chapter 12

STRESS MANAGEMENT

Set aside, for a few moments, the whole concept of disaster mental health. Instead, ask yourself why anyone, anywhere, would want to be a crisis intervention (CI) worker in any emergency mental health context. Consider this crisis staffer's description of his or her work (Weaver, 1984):

> Few others understand the nature and stresses . . . there's often a feeling of isolation. It is hard to leave the security of family life and enter a potentially dangerous, stressful situation. Crisis intervention can be emotionally and physically exhausting. It is rarely appreciated and not financially rewarding. Law enforcement officers, hospital personnel, and [consumers'] families can be uncooperative and verbally abusive, at times, in addition to confused by the law and misunderstanding of a [worker's duties]. Return to normalcy can be difficult after handling a crisis. (p. 14)

No matter what the context, a CI career is often quite physically and emotionally demanding for those who tackle it. CI workers report sleep difficulties, headaches, indigestion, more frequent colds, and even bowel difficulties and nausea, all due to the stress of their jobs (Resnik, H.L. Ruben, & D.D. Ruben, 1975; Weaver, 1984).

So why does anyone undertake (or stay with) a CI career? Many CI workers do tend to be the type of people who might best be characterized as crisis junkies. Life never seems to get wild and crazy enough for them, so they seek out ways to explore (and attempt to help resolve) the high-stress lives of other people in crisis. CI gets their adrenalin pumping and puts them at what many of them consider to be their optimal levels of performance.

The major difference from the rather negative scenario of CI (as quoted before) and DMH work is that disaster victims (and other helpers) are generally very grateful for the intervention efforts being offered to them. This, in turn, makes the work very emotionally rewarding to those who offer their services, especially if they are volunteering their time and expertise. Still, CI work in disasters is very stressful, and workers need to be aware of strategies that will help them prevent or control job-related stress and its sequelae.

PROVEN TECHNIQUES

The one best way to manage stress in disaster work is to find a coworker and develop an on-the-job support system. Ideally, one should never have to work on an assignment alone. Even if there are no other mental health workers or supervisors in the immediate area, there will usually be other relief workers with whom you can pair up. By using a buddy-system, workers can monitor each other for signs of stress, can routinely offer suggestions and support, and can defuse emotionally laden situations soon after they occur.

A survey of CI workers (Weaver, 1984) found that sharing with coworkers was the best method to manage stress, for both male and female workers. Sharing with supervisors, resting, reading, hobbies, and exercise were also rated as being effective. Less effective strategies were sharing with family members (perhaps due to fears that telling them about it would burden them or believing they could not relate to the work), and watching television or movies. Least effective, but too frequently used, were the crutches of alcohol consumption and smoking.

Another study by Bartone et al. (1989) found social supports seem to serve a protective function, helping insulate workers from many negative aspects of stress, particularly when the workers are faced with high exposure levels. They surmise this occurs because the presence of members of the support system "enhance[s] a sense of commitment to the [relief effort], thereby also diminishing the sense of role conflict and confusion" (p. 324).

Cultivating the skills necessary to manage stressful moments can be very helpful, too. First, you have to learn to recognize your personal warning signs. Often there is an easily discernible clue: a headache, an eye twitch, shoulder stiffness, an upset stomach, pain in the neck or in a joint, and so on. Once you make the determination that your early warning signal has sounded, you are ready to begin taking corrective action.

When you first notice things are becoming stressful, simple steps can often be of help immediately. One excellent method is to focus on your breathing. Take a few deep breaths, slowly inhaling and even more slowly exhaling each breath. This alone will help you relax and refocus your energy.

Similarly, you can do progressive muscle relaxation or some self-guided imagery. Paint a serene scene in your mind by spending some time thinking about a day at the beach, or a sunset, or another pleasant memory. If your imagination does not help, focus on some aspect of your environment (e.g., a sunny sky or an animal) for a bit. These kinds of minor distractions (minibreaks) can be very helpful. CMHS's (1988b) pamphlet, *Prevention and Control of Stress Among Emergency Workers: A Pamphlet for Workers*, offers these additional suggestions:

1. Let coworkers know when they are showing signs of fatigue and suggest they take a break. Have them do the same for you and listen to them when they clue you to the need for some rest. Tired workers lose their effectiveness.
2. Offer words of encouragement and support to others on the job. Recognize that there may be anger and criticism at times, but try to keep things on a positive note.
3. Tell others things like, "You are really doing a nice job!" and "I like the way you handled that situation!" Do the same thing for yourself with positive self-talk.
4. Keep yourself fed, get some exercise, and get the amount of sleep that you need to be at your best. Watch out for your eating behavior. There are always a lot of junk foods and sweets available, and people under stress may tend to eat and drink more than they usually would at home. It is fairly common for individuals with healthy appetites to gain weight while on assignment. Others who lose their appetites when under stress may also lose

weight. I know a woman who lost 10 pounds during her first DMH assignment.

5. Stay in touch with family and friends, especially while on assignments far from home. Write or call often. ARC encourages (and even reimburses) safe-arrival calls, weekly calls, and calls whenever a worker is moved to a new location.

6. Take time for the small things that help you relax when you are not working on a disaster. These might include reading, taking a bath, getting your hair done, listening to music, taking a walk, taking pictures, shopping, watching television, using your computer, or catching a nap.

7. Make new friends and spend time with them. Go out to eat, jog, shop, golf, bowl, or to the movies. Spend some breaks and time off together.

8. If you will be out in the field a long time, make your living quarters a nice, livable "home away from home" by unpacking (rather than living out of your suitcase), setting up some pictures of loved ones, and arranging things in the room so that it will be as comfortable for you as possible during the short periods of waking time you will spend there.

The same CMHS pamphlet (1988b) also suggests keeping a journal; I found that to be an excellent idea. I kept one during my first ARC disaster assignment. I started writing on the plane trip from Pennsylvania to Florida and kept it up throughout my trip. So much was happening so fast, from the moment I had first received the call, that I feared I might forget details that I wanted to be sure I had available to me for future use in training others who might volunteer. Although I started the journal almost as a chore or a bookkeeping function (anticipating one day writing a book about my experiences), I soon found that it worked extremely well as a method for processing and defusing stressful events at times when others were not around.

This journal does not have to be written in great detail, or kept in a special volume that will become one more thing you need to carry around with you. I simply use my pocket calendar that has lots of space for daily entries and has special pages or sections that can be added for additional notes. Those with laptop computers can use them to keep track of their thoughts and feelings while on the job. Find a way to make it fun and easy and, before you know it, you will be surprised how effective it can be.

DMH workers need to constantly be watching out for others who are not practicing the basic elements of stress management on their own behalf. Supervisors and other individuals in leadership roles are often the worst offenders. Despite being exposed to the same stressful conditions that are present in disasters, and having macrolevel responsibility for the relief operation, leaders will often overextend themselves by working without proper rest (Williams, Solomon, & Bartone, 1988). Others will need to encourage them to slow down and take proper care of themselves.

MAINTAINING A SENSE OF HUMOR

Lots of stress can be relieved by the effective use of a little bit of good-natured fun. Almost as quickly as a relief site opens, items such as cartoons, bogus forms, and top-10 lists (such as David Letterman's regular bit) begin circulating between the victims and the workers. Some of the best I have seen in recent months were:

1. An editorial cartoon that was posted in ARC headquarters in the Quad Cities during the Mississippi River/Midwest floods that, I believe, originally had appeared in a Deluth newspaper showed an "Updated Map of the United States," with "Lake Mississippi"at its center and Iowa floating off into the Gulf of Mexico; prominent on the map was an arrow pointing to Iowa with the caption, "You are here!"

2. A fake ARC form called "Requisition for Sleep" — the form, which appears on almost every job, cautions:

   During a disaster, sleep is available in a limited supply. Please do not request more than you need. Every effort will be made to fill your request; however, since sleep is given in limited quantities, we may not be able to fill your request. Any sleep

longer than the amount requested will be de-
ducted from your next request. Any sleep not
used is your loss and cannot be added to your next
request.

Of course the form says that requests have to be approved
by three supervisors in order to be valid.
3. A "Dennis the Menace" cartoon by artist Hank Ketcham
in which Dennis's Mom is picking up his toys and Dennis is saying, "If my room's such a big disaster area . . .
why don't ya call the Red Cross. Isn't that their business?" I have been unable to track down information
about when and where that cartoon originally appeared
in print.

Two first-time workers whom I recruited at the time of the
1994 Los Angeles earthquake returned with news of a unique,
homemade geologic instrument they had seen in an ARC setting. It consisted of a pancake dangling on a string, to form a
pendulum, and it was labeled *"Don't eat (seismograph)."* Next
to it was this finely calibrated scale — *"1 2 3 4 GET OUT."*

Just be careful about where you are, and what you are saying and doing, when you are having a good time. Victims do
retain their sense of humor, and many will poke fun of themselves and the messes they find themselves facing. Still, they
may take offense if they are coming into a relief center in order
to get help with their serious problems and they find the staff
there having what appears to be too good a time.

Gallows humor, on the other hand, is inappropriate in the
working environment or when relaxing. In fact, it is a common
warning sign of burnout, our next topic.

BURNOUT

Yes, it can happen to you! It happens to the best of workers.
We all want to do everything we can possibly do to help as many
people as we can manage to meet and serve. Sometimes we get
carried away. We push ourselves to the limits of physical and
psychological endurance, and then we try to do just a little bit
more. The result is burnout — "a state of exhaustion, irritability,

and fatigue, which may creep up on [us] . . . unrecognized and undetected" (Farberow, 1978b, p. 8).

Several factors can positively or negatively impact upon the likelihood of a serious stress response that might eventually lead to burnout. Some of them are the nature of the disaster, the workload, overall health, preexisting stresses (both in the individual helpers and in the helping organizations), prior ability to cope with stress, DMH experience and/or familiarity with previous stress events that were similar, identity issues and self-expectations, and the effectiveness of one's own safety net and/or social support system (Myers, 1985).

Once burnout has occurred, we lose our capability to carry on business as usual; our effectiveness is lessened. We often do not realize it, but we are no longer functioning with our usual skills and abilities intact. The problem often begins with lateness, avoidance of work, or loss of enthusiasm. The job no longer seems rewarding. Burned-out workers may even begin blaming the victims and viewing them as the cause of their own problems (Hartsough, 1985).

Several authors (Farberow, 1978a, 1978b, 1978d; Farberow & Gordon, 1981; Hartsough, 1985; Myers, 1985) list these warning signs of a stress response and possible burnout:

Thinking	Feeling
confused thinking	depression
difficulty making decisions	at a loss for energy
slowness of thought	anxiety
lack of alertness	excitability
trouble prioritizing work	low frustration tolerance
loss of objectivity	mood swings
suspect harm to self/others	overwhelmed
identification with victims	grief

Behavior	Physiological
crying spells	exhausted
overly active	limited energy
restless	stomach problems
socially withdrawn	loss of appetite
difficulty speaking/writing	trouble sleeping
sexual problems	trembling or tics

Behavior *(Cont'd)*	**Physiological** *(Cont'd)*
substance abuse	hypochondria
hypervigilance	frequent urination
gallows humor	impaired immune system

Another nasty wrinkle that appears with burnout is that the sufferers often feel that they are the only workers who can do their jobs; they tend to believe things will collapse if they do not carry on with their assignments themselves.

Here are some suggestions for handling burnout:

1. **Try To Catch It Early**. Know the symptoms and, once they spotted, take remedial action immediately. Teach others what to watch for as they begin their job assignments. Get into the habit of watching others and asking them to watch you.
2. **Ease Up**. People experiencing any of the common warning signs need to slow down. Reassess and reprioritize your work schedule. Ask for help if you are becoming overwhelmed. Somehow, you have to lower the level of stress.
3. **Involve Supervisory Personnel.** A supervisor needs to know if someone under his or her chain of command is burning out. Then, the supervisor needs to meet with the person, clearly explain the loss of efficiency (and the risks in not easing the stress), and come up with a plan to correct the situation. Possible actions may include taking more breaks, having some time off, or lessening official duties and responsibilities.
4. **Sometimes People Have to Be Sent Home**. In extreme cases, individuals may need to be totally relieved of duty and sent home. Leaving in this way is not something anyone enjoys having to do. Farberow notes, "any guilt in the worker over leaving is prevented by [his or her supervisor] giving official permission to stop" (1978b, p. 10). This needs to be accompanied by a reassuring discussion about why this must happen and how it will benefit the worker and those he or she was trying so hard to help.

Chapter 13

WORKING
WITH THE MEDIA

Having accurate and timely information about the disaster and the recovery is empowering to victims and helpers alike. The use of media contacts makes it very easy to convey psychoeducational messages to the public, and to do so quickly and efficiently. Part of the DMH workers' role is often to provide information to representatives of the broadcast and print media about such topics as the normal psychological effects of disasters on victims and helpers; stress management; grief, loss, and bereavement issues; phases of recovery; and the availability of DMH resources and services.

Although some of you may find it difficult to be taken seriously as an expert in your own hometown, expert status is rather quickly conferred by the residents of the disaster zone and by the local and national media operating at the scene. Reporters tend to be very impressed by those of us who are willing to take time out from our lives and travel to the disaster area to do this kind of work. This section will examine some of the products and pitfalls of serving as a media consultant.

POTENTIAL FOR
EMBARRASSMENT

Working with the media can present several challenges to the uninitiated DMH worker. Anything that can possibly go wrong will go wrong. The media will invariably pick up the least eloquent and/or intellectual statement that you make, and that is what they will most likely turn into the headline, or the 30-second sound bite, that will be repeated over and over again. Once you accept that fact and learn to exercise caution, you will do well when in the spotlight.

For instance, I was asked if I would allow a photographer from a local newspaper to come out to my primary place of employment on the day before I left for my ARC Mississippi/Midwest flood assignment for a sendoff story. It seemed that I was the first local ARC volunteer to go out from our area, so I said okay. The next morning, I was getting ready for work (sitting in the bathroom) and I was listening to the radio news. All of a sudden I heard that I was having a press conference at my office at 10:00 a.m. It was a moving experience!

The designated hour rolled around and instead of one photographer, two television station camera crews and reporters from two radio stations and two newspapers arrived ready for a press conference. For the next 90 minutes or so, my office became a small-scale media circus. For most of that time, I was doing a fairly decent job. I spoke rather eloquently about disaster operations in general, about DMH interventions, about prevention of PTSD, and even about ARC's need to urgently recruit more volunteers and raise more money for relief supplies.

At one point I was asked why I (or anyone) would want to leave the safety and security of my job, home, and family, and travel far away to a disaster site to do this kind of work. Well, I went on for at least 5 minutes about how much CI and disaster workers enjoy dealing with the unknown stresses inherent in this kind of situation. What did they all find to be the most interesting thing I said? A brief, joking statement I made near the end of my discourse on the joys of DMH work—the only joke I made, in fact, during the whole interview—that I was a crisis junkie who, like others of my genre, thrive on the stress. Although this is true, of course, it was not what I had hoped to hear highlighted from the interview.

Things worked out well after all. The media splash when I left, continued coverage while I was on assignment, and another interview upon my return all helped raise lots of money and was instrumental in recruitment of dozens of volunteers.

There have been other times that my DMH coverage has caused me problems. My graduate degree is in social work, but some reporters make a habit of calling me a psychologist, possibly because my undergraduate degree is in psychology and I sometimes teach psychology at our local community college.

There must be an inaccurate bio on me filed somewhere, because I cannot seem to get that corrected.

My friends hassle me about my "celebrity status" every time I get mentioned in the local media. One man, a former supervisor, asked me for $3 upon my return from the Mississippi/Midwest flood zone. He said I took up at least $3 worth of space in his morning paper while I was away, he was tired of hearing about me, and he wanted a rebate.

The worst, though, was that DMH publicity actually resulted in higher taxes for me. It seems that, where I live, there is someone whose role in life is to read the papers looking for anything that will result in a change to the township's tax roles. One of the articles listed me as a casework supervisor, and the operative word there was supervisor. That part of the title meant I had won the right to pay higher per capita taxes — just another perk earned through DMH volunteering and effective use of the media.

Actually, as you might have guessed, it is all a lot of fun. I am simply warning you that interviews you give can have many unintended results. With that in mind, here are several useful tips on working with the media.

PRACTICAL TIPS

1. **Be sure to weigh your words before you deliver your message.** You can always add to a statement you have made to the media, but you cannot easily take part of it back.
2. **Be positive and upbeat — convey a message of hope.** Tell people about the availability of relief programs and where to find whatever services you may describe. Squelch any rumors and try to correct any previously circulated misinformation. Victims need to know that help has arrived and that order is being restored. This will help them regain a sense of control over their lives.
3. **Use the prepared materials.** There is no need to generate new information on the spot — you will have enough work to do as it is. Instead, rely upon the prepackaged materials and the wealth of available resources from previous, similar disasters. CMHS's pamphlet *The Media in*

a Disaster (Farberow, 1978c) contains sample press releases and radio spots. ARC has similar boilerplate releases. Keep samples from job to job and tailor them to
fit your needs. Use information from this book and/or
listed references.

4. **Stress the normal reactions to disasters.** It is very reassuring to people to hear that it is okay to feel bad in the
wake of a disaster. Allay their fears about the rush of
strange thoughts, feelings, and emotions which they are
suddenly experiencing. Let them know they are not becoming mentally ill on top of everything else they have
been through.

5. **Inoculate the public to the stress of predictable future
events.** Teach them, via the media, about the phases of
recovery, anniversary reactions, and so on. The more they
are able to understand the process, the less scary it will
be. By the way, Myers (1994) contains a chapter on anniversary reactions, which will be very helpful if you are
asked to provide information about that phenomenon.

6. **Work with supervisory staff and with the public affairs
component of your organization.** ARC, for instance, has
a large and very active public affairs department that can
provide guidelines for your media contacts. The public
affairs people will also have the statistical information
(How many deaths? Number of people fed? Sheltered?
Etc.) that the media likes to include as part of any story.

7. **The media craves sensational stories**. Reporters will
press you for detailed case examples. Be careful to protect the confidentiality and privacy of those victims and
helpers whose stories you may be tempted to share.
Jacobs et al. (1990) caution that the best way to avoid accidental breeches of confidentiality or the inadvertent
sharing of inaccurate information is to have all interviews
be handled through a designated spokesperson.

8. **It can't hurt to ask.** Remember, too, that once you have
the spotlight, it never hurts to do a little bit of public relations work. Ask for more donations and more volunteers; recent disasters have been so large that it seems
there can never be enough of either one. Requesting and
receiving needed *in-kind gift* items (such as crayons, toys,

bug spray, etc.), cash donations, and fresh, new recruits can really help at most disaster scenes.

Although I have never accompanied anyone from the media on any of his or her jaunts through a disaster scene, I suspect that doing so would provide yet another suitable intervention opportunity for DMH workers. I say that because I have spent some time traveling with a film crew that was developing new training materials for ARC.

I took the crew to see a family with whom I had worked earlier in the week of the crew's visit. With the written permission of the two victims, the crew shot some excellent footage of them describing their losses and their efforts to clean up and repair their badly damaged home. The victims broke down in tears and said some things that caused strong reactions from the film crew. It was the first time one of the family members had cried about her losses, and the other family member was glad it had finally happened. During the shoot, I spent time defusing the family. After the shoot, I found myself defusing the two crew people about this visit and about several earlier ones.

One final bit of advice is in order. When dealing with the media, it is a good practice to give some advance thought to the ethical issues inherent in entering the interview process. You will be serving in a relief role that, at the time of the interview, has public education and stress-inoculation as its primary objectives. Although some degree of secondary gain may naturally occur in our behalf because of our media exposure, DMH workers must avoid any temptation to undertake media contacts as a means to overtly advertise our private practices or seek personal recognition.

Chapter 14

HEADING HOME FROM A DISASTER

The need for rest is the primary concern for most workers following a disaster. By the closing days of an assignment, most people feel exhausted, both mentally and physically. Workers may not appreciate how tired they are until something unusual happens that draws attention to the need for a break. As an example, here is a journal entry written by a DMH colleague of mine toward the end of his first long assignment (David Hankard, personal communication, February 19, 1994):

> At supper [another first time DMH worker and I] have great difficulty trying to figure out details of sharing a car [for our half-days off]. Finally, we use the bread basket (as the car), salt and pepper shakers as [the two of us], and silverware as geographic points to figure this out. It would seem we are suffering from some kind of mental confusion.

The next day, when both workers were rested, a better carpooling plan came to them rather easily and, in retrospect, the whole event seemed quite silly.

It is hard to get the rest you need while on a long assignment, and it is important to do some catching up once it is all over. Take it easy for a couple of days, and get the needed rest! Sounds simple and easy, right? If only that were the case.

Family members, your friends, the work that has piled up at your job, and the routine chores that may have gone undone (like planting or weeding the garden), are all lined up and waiting to pounce on you, to demand your immediate attention once you arrive home. How can anyone think about resting when there is so much to do? Balancing the essential need for rest with the demands of others and your own desire to quickly catch up on everything is probably the greatest challenge you will face during the process of returning home from an assignment.

Flynn (1987) offers these additional hints on what to expect once you arrive at home:

1. The pace of activity at a disaster is usually quite a bit faster than the normal pace of things at home or at work. Consequently, you may still be moving in the fast lane, wanting to zip through many things. As you speed along, you may find yourself becoming annoyed at everyone else because others seem to be moving at a snail's pace. Relax and slow down! Theirs is the normal pace.

2. You probably will want to talk about the memories of your experiences at length with family members and friends. Some people will be happy to listen and will be genuinely interested; some will be polite, but not appear very attentive (or possibly they are simply unable to relate to the situation); and some will be far more concerned with telling you what they have been doing while you were away. Realizing that these are all typical reactions, and being attuned to others' needs as well as your own, will help everyone better manage their discussing desires.

3. Sometimes the need to avoid talking about recent events is also a distinct possibility. Some people are not ready to tell their story immediately upon their return home. This is most common when workers are very tired or when things were so emotionally charged that they will need more time to process whatever happened before they can share it. People also may vacillate between wanting and not wanting to talk about things, just as disaster victims vary in their willingness to talk about their ordeal. These are all considered normal reactions.

4. There is also a good chance you will ride on a rollercoaster of emotions during the days following your return home. You may feel disappointment that the reunion did not go as well as expected, or possibly feel frustrated at demands others (or you) have placed on your time and energy. You may become easily angered at people at home

whose little problems seem to pale in comparison to the serious issues facing the victims you had been helping.

5. Those of you with children will also need to help them understand where you were, what kind of work you were doing, some idea about the damage that occurred, and why you are interested in doing this type of work. The key is to present the information to children in a way that will satisfy their curiosity without scaring them. I have found that showing my two young children my pictures, watching television news accounts with them, and directly telling them about my experiences seems to work well.

Flynn (1987) concludes his article with a brief commentary about using the days and weeks immediately following your disaster assignment as an opportunity for introspection and a review of personal growth that probably has occurred because of the experience. My guess is that most of you will also spend some time thinking about when and how you can get out and do it again.

ARC has developed a series of excellent educational brochures for staff and victims. One of the best, *Coping With Disaster: Returning Home from a Disaster Assignment* (ARC, 1991), addresses these same physical and emotional issues. Every ARC worker gets one as he or she is leaving a field assignment.

One final note about returning home: Try not to lose your return ticket. On one job I had to get a new ticket because I got to the airport very close to flight time and could not find my ticket. I was accustomed to keeping it in one place in my briefcase whenever I traveled but, for some reason, I had accidentally moved it to a different piece of luggage. Fortunately, the ARC travel agency got me a new one in time. When I got home, I found the original and sent it to the travel agency; they were able to rectify everything without any lost money. Moral of the story — be careful with those little last-minute details that are needed to get you home. As embarrassing as this story is to tell, I wanted to warn readers that by the end of your assignment you will be very physically and mentally tired, as I was, and you will be more apt to make careless mistakes.

Chapter 15

SUPERVISORY ISSUES

During graduate school I focused much of my elective course work on issues of supervision and administration. One of my favorite authors to cite in presentations or papers was Alfred Kadushin. He has written many articles and books that seem to delineate clearly and simply the core issues needed to begin our discussion of DMH supervision.

There are many obvious reasons that supervision is needed in any situation where services are being delivered to hundreds (or even thousands) of people via huge, bureaucratic organizations. Kadushin (1976) names several factors that have traditionally dictated the need for effective supervision in any large human service endeavor, including:

- helping assess need
- enhancing overall efficiency
- monitoring and reviewing worker performance
- interpreting policy issues
- meeting uniform standards of service delivery
- assuring accountability for expenditure of resources

Accomplishing all these things will be difficult even under the best of managerial circumstances, and disaster zones seldom represent ideal situations in which to work.

With the nature of disaster work being what it is, large numbers of DMH professionals (and people from all other areas of specialization) are drawn together from different walks of life. They appear, put in their tours of duty, and return home, only to be replaced by other new workers. They usually have not trained together and many may be inexperienced. They have a variety of perspectives on how to best preform their functions. Like the rest of us, they are products of heredity and environment, and will show a variety of moods, personality traits, skill levels, and methods of coping with stress. Hopefully, they all will at least share the common goal of helping the victims get back on their feet.

One of the greatest challenges you will face in DMH supervision is tapping the talents of the pool of volunteer professionals fate deals you and gelling them into an effective corps of field operatives who can carry on an effective, autonomous practice. This, sadly, is the case because there still are not enough trained and willing DMH workers to fully meet the need. Rather than be able to assign two workers to each service center or shelter (to balance in-house concerns with outreach), there is often a need to have one worker ride a circuit among several service sites.

Kadushin (1976) goes on to outline three primary types of supervision:

- *Administrative*—supervision that guides the day-to-day activities of the workers, including assigning duties, directing activity, and evaluating work performance.
- *Educational*—supervision that provides an initial job orientation and then adds any ongoing training that may be needed to enhance a workers' knowledge base, skills, and abilities.
- *Supportive*—supervision that monitors and, whenever possible, meets the workers' job-related emotional needs.

A supervisory style that utilizes a combination of all three types of supervision seems especially well suited as a model for DMH managers.

ADMINISTRATIVE TASKS AND CHALLENGES

Supervisory staff must take on many challenges besides the obvious tasks required to direct, train, and support the frontline workers. Here is a partial overview of the managerial activities with which you may become involved in a typical DMH operation.

INITIAL SETUP

Start-up tasks include checking out the disaster area and getting a preliminary assessment of the scope of the damage and the needs of the victims; estimating the number and type of workers that will be required; beginning to think about the logistical needs of those people (such as assuring there will be adequate housing, vehicles, supplies, and work space); assessing the environmental stressors and personal safety risks that may be present for the helpers; and beginning to work with the many people from other specializations who will help organize the full response.

NETWORKING

Additional aspects of start-up include making contacts with the local officials, public and private providers of inpatient and outpatient treatment services, crisis intervention units, other human service agencies, and professional organizations (NASW, APA, ACA, AAMFT, etc.); obtaining and/or developing a list of referral resources; getting to know the others within the advance team of your own sponsoring organization to lay a firm foundation for later working relationships; and maintaining all these lists, contacts, and relationships over the full extent of the job.

RECRUITMENT/SCREENING/TRAINING

Once the scope of the job has been determined, activities switch to getting the initial group of workers out; providing them with an initial orientation and ongoing information and support; keeping abreast of workers' tours of duty that are ending and the need for replacements; and monitoring workers as they enter (and leave) the job, in order to be sure they are up to the challenges that lie ahead. There is also a need to verify the credentials (licenses or certifications) of DMH workers as they arrive.

In some instances, time must be spent recruiting and training local volunteers to bolster the pool of available DMH workers. Articles by Heffron (1977), Zarle, Hartsough, and Ottinger

(1974), Myers (1994), and material contained in many of the CMHS publications can be of great help in training professionals and paraprofessionals. All emphasize that you can save a great deal of time during start-up if you have a plan in place before a disaster strikes.

Anticipate frustration from some new people who volunteer their time and are then asked to undergo required DMH (or other specialty) training before they are assigned to the job. Many professionals feel that their careers have provided them the background and skills they will need for a disaster assignment. They expect to be placed into immediate service and resent having to be screened and be given further training before ARC (or other organizations) will be willing and able to use their services.

FIELD ASSIGNMENTS/DEPLOYMENT

Supervisors must be alert to the staffing needs of the various service locations and to the personalities, practice styles, strengths, and weaknesses of the many DMH workers on the job; and assigning or transferring people accordingly.

SUPERVISION

Administrative personnel must maintain regular contact with the members of the field staff in order to oversee their work, communicate information from headquarters, answer questions, assign and review tasks, provide support, and evaluate their job performance. Sometimes it will mean exploring and documenting problems, working to alleviate them, and sending workers home when corrective action is not possible.

LOGISTICS

Managers must keep on top of the many, ongoing details of housing, transportation, and working conditions—things that can easily make or break a worker's job effectiveness (and positively or negatively influence his or her willingness to come out on any future assignments).

BALANCING NEEDS OF STAFF
WITH NEEDS OF COMMUNITY

In an ideal world there would be enough workers to meet all the mental health needs of both the survivors and the relief workers; in the real world, resources are finite, and effort must be made to assist both groups with the limited number of DMH workers that may be available. In the process, be careful that you do not allow (or require) workers to overtax themselves. Monitor time on the job and enforce use of breaks and time off.

POLITICS, POWER, AND AUTHORITY

Anyone who has been an elected public figure, or who has worked in a public sector human service setting, needs no further explanation of these factors. For those who have not done so, here are several other situations that may help illustrate these touchy concepts: being an officer or board member of any organization from a Parent Teacher Association to a nonprofit agency; trying to settle a dispute between your spouse and your kids, when privately you are siding with the kids; or almost everything that bothered you about graduate school and/or a former job. The minister at my church often says that a good way to put one's faith to the test is to become a member of consistory (the governing body). All of this is meant to caution supervisors that they need to keep a close watch over hundreds of little things that can, in an instant, become big things capable of tearing an operation (and even an organization) apart.

PUBLIC RELATIONS

To understand this issue, see politics, power, and authority (above) but add the element of public scrutiny over almost every aspect of what is being said and done. Supervisors need to carefully monitor DMH activities in order to assure public acceptance and confidence in the DMH staff members and in the organization you represent.

RECORD KEEPING/STATISTICS

Few people in the business of helping people enjoy the **bean-counting** functions of their jobs. Nevertheless, we need to keep track of what we are doing, and with whom we are doing it, in order to make a responsible accounting to our sponsoring organizations. These figures are also essential for public relations and for planning the relief operations.

FUTURE PLANNING

A critical element of each job is the ongoing task of reviewing the current job with an eye to future improvements. Supervisory staff gather feedback about the job and encourage staff members to share with them the aspects of the DMH function that are working well and those aspects that need further refinement. At the end of each job, ARC supervisors write narrative reports that summarize areas of strengths and needs. They usually encourage all their staff members to do the same, as each leaves the job.

SELECTION OF WORK LOCATIONS

Something with which managers will sometimes become involved is the selection of work sites for service centers and shelters. Although there is little time to shop around, and there is not always a large variety of facilities from which to choose, there are factors to keep in mind whenever possible. The guidelines for amount of space, number of bathrooms, and so on, per size of victim population are well documented and available elsewhere. My interest here is more in the mental health aspects of site selection.

In ARC, it is fairly common to work in several locations on each job—there just are not enough of us yet. On my first job, I was briefly assigned to a very large service center that was housed in a fire station garage. The trucks had been pulled out, and splintered, old, rented tables and chairs were put in; our furniture looked bad, and it felt even worse than it looked. The room was large, hot, poorly lit, and lined with typical fire equipment (bells, hoses, ladders, axes, oxygen bottles, boots, etc.); all the fire and rescue trucks were parked just outside.

This was an unpleasant working environment, filled with many visual artifacts that would tend to raise stress levels among those who may well have seen this equipment before, during the rescue efforts immediately following the disaster. Thankfully, the sirens did not go off while I was there. My total stay there was less than 2 hours before headquarters notified me that I was in greater need at another location.

I was then transferred to a smaller service center that had managed to obtain space in the reading room of a library. It was air-conditioned, had better tables, had padded chairs, had carpeting, and the room was lined with attractive bookshelves filled with books and magazines. A small canteen with fruit, cookies, drinks, and other snack foods was set up just inside the front door. What a switch! Where the first location seemed to ooze a stressful message of pain and suffering, this one seemed to have a tranquilizing effect upon everyone who entered the site.

The people in the first location (victims and workers) were visibly more stressed than the people in the second. I had no more than entered the first location when someone accused me of stealing his favorite chair. Minutes later, another worker started complaining to me about some of her coworkers. The managers were even at odds over allowing children to have crayons in the center. At the second location none of this kind of behavior was going on. Coincidence? I don't think so.

Clearly, we cannot always pick an ideal space like that library. In fact, on many assignments the fire station garage would have seemed like paradise. In the Hurricane Andrew relief effort, for instance, work was often carried out in large, very hot military tents. Nevertheless, workers need to be made aware of the dramatic effects that the work environment can have on the productivity and morale of the staff, and on the general mood of the victims who are being seen there.

In our own practices, we try to set up our offices in a way that offers a safe, comfortable, and peaceful environment. To whatever degree possible, we need to try to do the same thing when we are on relief assignments. If you are helping with site selection, try to pick locations that better lend themselves to providing a low-stress experience. When you do not have an ideal location in which to work, be sure to search out some other, quiet spots (under a tree, in a car, etc.), somewhere apart from the grander stresses of the service center or shelter.

SUPERVISORY CONTACTS

During the ARC jobs in which I have served thus far, several approaches have been used for maintaining contact and providing supervisory support. Following is a brief description of each type.

DAILY CONTACTS

ARC requires daily reporting of statistics from each functional specialization. This means DMH workers need to be in contact with headquarters each day, if only to turn in their numbers. This regular call (or visit, if working nearby) allows a few minutes for supervisors to check workers' status, answer questions, resolve any outstanding matters from previous days, provide new information, monitor stress levels, and offer support.

GROUP MEETINGS BY FUNCTION

DMH workers in a regional area try to get together from time to time, for a meeting over supper. That way, they are not pulled away from a large portion of their workday, and even those who have some distance to travel can sometimes take part. Because of the time and travel involved, these generally occur only once during a 2- to 3-week tour of duty.

GROUP MEETINGS BY WORK SITE

Far more common than meetings by function, these often occur daily and come in two types: a formal, morning meeting and informal get-togethers. ARC service centers (and most other work sites) routinely have general staff meetings on a daily basis. These occur first thing in the morning, before the centers open to the public.

Announcements are made, new resources are shared, each specialty unit makes a brief report, and the staff members who are entering or leaving the job are recognized. These meetings help everyone immediately feel included as part of the team. They also provide a marvelous opportunity for DMH workers to monitor stress levels of everyone present and to make minipresentations on aspects of DMH like stress management.

During my first assignment, I worked primarily in a small service center, and we had these meetings daily. Staff really looked forward to them. We enjoyed the jump-start this mix of statistics, the news from headquarters, the staff introductions, the farewell speeches, and even some comedy would give us each morning.

On my second assignment I worked in a field headquarters office. There, staff meetings were not held daily, and those that were held were only for the top administrative personnel. The other workers who were left out (all people who were accustomed to having daily meetings) and I found we greatly missed the morning sessions, the information they would have shared, and the camaraderie they would typically have generated.

The informal get-togethers occur spontaneously, as staff members from various specializations get together over breakfast or dinner. These social gatherings are also very helpful for monitoring stress levels and providing peer support.

SITE VISITS BY SUPERVISORS

When possible, the DMH supervisors will make field trips from headquarters, riding a circuit and visiting DMH staff in the service centers and shelters. How often these occur will depend upon how large a territory needs to be covered, whether other DMH staff members are available to handle DMH functions at headquarters while the supervisor is on the road, and how pressing the need is for face-to-face supervisory contacts.

SITE VISITS BY OTHER DMH STAFF

When supervisors cannot get out to do field visits, sending other DMH staff, even first-timers, can be equally effective in terms of the support these visits can provide. The veteran worker in the service center or shelter can give the visiting worker a narrated tour of the disaster zone and explain his or her DMH activities. The visitor can, in turn, do some defusing and debriefing, offer support, and be learning at the same time. This seems to work equally well as a one-shot visit or as a briefing before turning over the assignment to a new worker whenever someone is going home.

Workers seem to find these visits especially helpful and supportive. I have enjoyed both receiving the visits and making them. Unfortunately, there often will not be enough people available to allow many site visits of either type to be made.

As I said at the beginning of this section, these examples are drawn from my ARC experiences. Making new friends and finding sources of both peer and supervisory supports are a big part of stress management in disaster relief work. All these approaches seem to work extremely well, and they can be easily adapted for use in other organizations.

FACTORS THAT INFLUENCE SUPERVISORY RELATIONSHIPS

Successful relationships between DMH supervisors and staff members seem to be contingent upon several factors. A few of the more important ones are:

1. *Availability.* Finding enough time in the supervisors' and supervisees' schedules to be able to carry out routine supervisory tasks. Achieving physical proximity to conduct a supervisory conference is difficult in disasters. Both parties are very busy, and there is often considerable distance between them. Lots of supervision ends up being done via telephone calls back and forth from headquarters.
2. *Approachability.* Getting a workable mix of managerial and learning styles, along with compatible personalities, tends to foster the development of positive relationships. A manager whose "door is always open" is sending the right message. So, too, is a worker who welcomes and seeks feedback on his or her job performance.
3. *Adaptability.* Willingness is needed on both sides of the relationship to openly discuss issues, engage in problem-solving activities, make any needed changes, and get on with the business of helping the victims. Disaster opera-

tions are difficult enough without the addition of defensive or obstreperous behavior by either party.

Other elements of managerial style are also critical to the success or failure of working relationships. Managers are part of the power structure of any organization. How they exercise that power can exert a major positive or negative influence over their subordinates and, consequently, over the functioning of the entire organization.

Kadushin (1976) talks about the five types of power that exist within an organization:

- *Reward Power*— the power to bestow blessings upon those who behave properly.
- *Coercive Power*— the ability to compel people to perform in a desired manner.
- *Legitimate (Positional) Power*— the power that comes with rank or is linked to positions of authority.
- *Referent (Relationship) Power*— which grows out of a desire to emulate someone in authority with whom the supervisee has a positive relationship.
- *Expert Power*— held because of special knowledge, skills, and abilities.

The first three types are considered *formal* power and are more often seen in administrative supervision. The latter two types are considered *functional* power and lend themselves more to educational and supportive supervision. DMH supervisors tend to rely more heavily upon their functional power.

Communication within an organization, both verbal and written, is often a reflection of managerial style. In most instances, the flow of information is best (most efficient) from the top down. Getting information back from the line workers to administration is harder. Workers may be reluctant to share information with a manager, especially if that information may reflect negatively on them or their peers. Bosses, on the other hand, may attempt to buffer (and protect) line workers from information that they feel would be upsetting to them. Supervisors need to constantly watch for things that might be barriers to effective communication (Kadushin, 1976).

SENSITIVITY AND SUPPORT

Being sensitive to workers' needs is another key part of supervision. Because a big part of the job involves being supportive of line workers, a review of several ways to provide verbal support is in order.

- *Positive Statements:*
  You are doing a great job.
  Keep up the good work.
  I like how you handled that situation.

- *Educational Statements:*
  Here is a technique I learned. . . .
  Have you thought about trying. . . ?
  I have read good things about the use of. . . .

- *Sanctioning Statements:*
  You are doing exactly what needs to be done.
  I wish more folks would do what you did.
  I'm with you (backing you) on this.

- *Statements That Show Recognition of Limits:*
  I know how hard you worked on this.
  People are trying to do their best.
  We can't always get everything accomplished.

- *Self-Disclosure Statements:*
  When I ran into that, I wanted to. . . .
  One time I felt like. . . .
  I once tried to. . . .

It is also helpful to share positive feedback you have received from others about one of your workers. Victims, coworkers, and other supervisors will sometimes make very flattering comments about someone you are supervising. Be sure to pass the compliments along to the workers and, if possible, work them into your evaluations.

Supervisors can also be supportive in other ways. Be sure workers take breaks and get some time off. Rotate assignments that are especially stressful or especially boring. Check to be sure workers are finding and using sources of social support on the job and that they are keeping in touch with those persons who are going to be their support system when they get back home.

One final note of caution—supervision should not evolve into therapy (Kadushin, 1976). It is a common practice to use supervisory interviews as a means to bring troublesome issues to the surface in order to enhance workers' self-awareness. The trick is to keep an educational perspective rather than a clinical one. Therapeutic issues need to be handled in therapy. There is enough to be done at a disaster scene without crossing this line in supervision.

HELPING WORKERS
CLOSE OUT THEIR ASSIGNMENTS

Supervisors need to help their workers bring closure to their tours of duty. Here are some of the related tasks:

1. **Have each worker review material on heading home from a disaster.** Key points were presented in an earlier section of this book and also appear in various other pamphlets and publications. Alert them to any specific issues you feel they may encounter.
2. **Be sure workers have an opportunity to defuse whatever tension has built up during their stay.** Have them tell you about the most troublesome aspects of their assignment, how they managed stress, and their success stories. Encourage them to attend a more formal debriefing, now or when they get home, if one is available.
3. **Make sure workers' specific job tasks have been completed.** Have needed referrals been made? Is all necessary paperwork completed and turned in? If new workers are going into the same sites, have they had a chance to meet with the outgoing workers?
4. **Get workers' input on their jobs, as they experienced them.** Have workers write a brief narrative highlighting the best and the worst aspects of their assignments. Try to get suggestions for improvement of things that they disliked. It is also a good idea to constantly gather information for your own narrative as you go through your tour of duty. Try to capture and document any and all ideas that might help make future assignments better for everyone.

5. **Conduct an evaluation of workers' performance.** Because of the nature of disaster work, you may have to rely heavily upon input from others who were able to better observe the individuals in question. Whenever possible, include both the workers and the other observers (preferably supervisors or job directors) in the process, so that workers can directly receive the feedback and are allowed an opportunity to respond.

6. **Relieve them of their duties early enough to allow a smooth release from the job.** Then, have them make sure all the paperwork needed to leave for home is getting done in a timely manner. Otherwise, workers may find themselves hung up in red tape at the time they attempt to make their exit. These matters can include checking out of hotels, settling travel vouchers, rental-car returns, and many other last minute stressors.

WHY EMERGENCY TEAMS
MAY SOMETIMES FAIL

Parad et al. (1975a) caution that even the best of teams may sometimes experience failure. Here are some of the possible reasons they give for why things might go wrong.

INADEQUATE PLANNING

Sometimes a key element is missed in designing or executing the disaster response plan. This can disrupt critical functions such as triage. DMH workers may find themselves badly understaffed, poorly trained, inadequately briefed, or improperly deployed. All of this can lead to a sense of paralysis in which "the team members end up dissipating their energies in many different directions, and few people, if any, are adequately handled" (Parad et al., 1975a, p. 15).

PERSONAL REACTIONS
INTERFERE WITH EFFECTIVENESS

Disaster situations are not for everyone. Sometimes workers misjudge their interests and/or tolerance levels and find out after they are already on the job that DMH work is not for them. Other times the workers may simply get in way over their heads — "team members [can become] so overwhelmed by the physical aspects of an emergency that they fail to deal with the psychological aspects" (p. 15). A third possibility is that workers feel okay about the disaster but let other personal issues cloud their judgment in the handling of their cases. The example they cite is that of a worker with a substance abuse problem. That worker can be "blinded by his [or her] emotions so that it is impossible to make an appropriate assessment or develop a disposition" (p. 15). Victims and the workers, themselves, suffer when this occurs.

DMH PROBLEMS ARE SEEN BUT INADEQUATELY ADDRESSED

Team members sometimes manage to properly recognize and identify the psychological issues of victims or fellow workers, but do not adequately handle them. They point out that this often occurs when "staff members attempt to function beyond the limits of their own expertise, failing to seek consultation and making inappropriate dispositions" (p. 15).

LACK OF FOLLOW-UP CARE

Referrals are made but not followed up to be sure connections were made between the victims (or workers) and the service providers to whom they were referred. Even when individuals have been connected with the providers, it is prudent to continue to monitor some situations, especially if the case scenario involves a worker who is staying on the job while receiving treatment.

Chapter 16

FURTHER EVOLUTION OF DISASTER MENTAL HEALTH

Upon returning from his first major assignment, one of my DMH colleagues characterized the work by saying, "basically we are troubleshooters . . . [our role] could be as simple as thinking to turn on the overhead fans when people are getting hot, or sitting in during volatile interviews" (David Hankard, personal communication, February 19, 1994). As his comment implies, our DMH function will not always involve us in intensely clinical practice of the type we may face in our day-to-day jobs. Nevertheless, when this kind of work is combined with the defusing/debriefing, the psychoeducation, and the crisis intervention services we do provide, DMH represents a very important component of a relief operation.

Although the main concepts of DMH have been in development for about 50 years, it is still a relatively new area of specialization for many relief organizations. For instance, ARC formally added its DMH component in the last 4 years. As this book nears publication, FEMA is working on developing a DMH program for its staff. CMHS is continuing to fund additional research projects designed to expand our knowledge base.

All DMH workers clearly have a shared responsibility to continue our efforts to document, debate, evaluate, and refine the various processes and techniques we use to help both the disaster victims and the helpers who provide relief services to them. The efficacy of our intervention strategies is one area of practice that is especially in need of evaluative research.

We also need to continue expanding our recruitment efforts and training opportunities. As I have noted over and over again, there simply are not enough of us to do the job. The Mississippi/Midwest floods and the Los Angeles earthquake have shown us how great DMH staffing needs can be. Yet we still have been quite lucky in that we have not been hit by a worse mass-casualty disaster in a major population center. Disaster planners fear the day when an Andrew-like storm surprises us and hits squarely the heart of a large city like Miami or New Orleans, or an earthquake strikes a city that has not been built to withstand such an assault.

Stimulating interest in new recruits, fostering the development of a skilled corps of workers, and continuing to intellectually challenge experienced workers, all will require new and better instructional materials. Many of the handouts and audiovisual presentations we currently have to offer are rather dry and lifeless. Thankfully, we have the "war stories" to keep things alive and vibrant. Those with a flair for writing and/or video production need to work with their organizations to improve the handouts, manuals, and training films.

Speaking of training films and recruitment, an excellent new ARC video, *You Do What You Have to Do — Stories from the Great Flood of '93* (ARC, 1994), has been released. It contains footage of many persons filmed both during the flood and when these same people were revisited several months later. It was produced by the film crew that I mentioned having assisted in the section on working with the media. The resulting 16-minute video portrays ARC workers in action as well as survivors who are getting on with their lives. Although it is not meant to be a DMH film, it is an excellent resource for enlisting others to join ARC and for illustrating some of the demanding, real-life drama that DMH workers will encounter.

Especially noticable in the tape are relief workers who extended themselves to the limits of their endurance by working long hours, for weeks at a time, without taking time off. The workers' dedication is matched by the fighting spirit shown by the survivors as they were struggling to reestablish their homes and their lifestyles. Toward the end of the film, an executive director of a Red Cross chapter exclaims, "I believe in the mission!" Anyone who joins us in future relief efforts will quickly discover what she means and feel the same way.

EPILOGUE

DMH — I love it! If you have taken the time to read this book, my guess is that you already love relief work as well, or you will love it once you become trained and get out on your first assignment. The experiences I have had thus far have been extremely rewarding. DMH work has led to the kinds of interactions I (and most of us in DMH) expected would be far more frequent occurrences when we entered our careers in the helping professions.

During 1994 I became a qualified ARC DMH instructor. I hope this means I may see some of you in future classes. Even though another year has passed since the original draft for this book was submitted, and many more DMH volunteers have been trained, there is still a shortage. ARC continues to offer the course as often as possible, all over the country. Special "fly and train" *(mobilization training)* classes have been added for recent events like the 1994 flooding which occurred in Alabama, Florida, and Georgia from Tropical Storm Alberto and from a series of storms which struck Texas later in the year. Make the call to ARC and get involved! You'll be glad you did.

When I find myself speaking before audiences who have invited me to talk about my ARC experiences, I can sense the growing excitement in some people — those who seem to have a budding interest in DMH. They listen intently to the stories I impart, and, by the end of the session, I can tell that they, too, have been caught by the same magical attraction this work holds for me and for so many of my colleagues. I have already managed to recruit several new DMH workers for ARC, and, when I cannot go out, I can still be of help by covering some of their duties here at home while they go on assignment.

As I said in the introduction, I hope this book will serve to generate interest among other newcomers and draw in a few more recruits. If you are one such person, I strongly urge you to make a call to ARC, to one of the many other VOAD member agencies/organizations, or to a CISD team. Sign up and become an active partner in future relief efforts.

For the rest of you veteran workers, I hope this book has proven to be a useful review and that maybe you have learned a thing or two about DMH that you did not previously know. Like me, you probably will not be able to go out on distant assignments as often as you may want to do so. My agreement with my wife is that I will go once a year (but I might get out twice, as I did my first year, if things are really bad at some future disaster).

Think about doing as I am doing, and channel some of your time, energy, and interest in DMH into the areas of preparedness planning, recruitment, training, and other local relief efforts of the various professional groups and disaster service organizations in your hometown. Or, try something new, from my list of other DMH opportunities. In this way you can continue to help throughout the year.

Many thanks to all of you for your interest in this book. Please feel free to write me with your comments, stories (successes or failures), and suggestions for additional DMH intervention strategies and techniques. Who knows? Maybe I can gather enough new material to generate a second volume.

Thanks for your interest in DMH. See you down the road.

John D. Weaver
4635 Hillview Drive
Nazareth, PA 18064-8531

APPENDICES

Appendix A

COMMONLY PRESCRIBED PSYCHOTROPIC MEDICATIONS

Workers doing DMH interventions will sometimes find themselves dealing with persons who are taking psychotropic medications. The following represents a partial list of brand-name medications, with the generic names in parentheses, and organized by the usage categories for which they are commonly prescribed. This list will help you properly identify (and spell) the names of the listed drugs. In addition, you will sometimes find that knowing the medication can also provide some clues as to the preexisting conditions for which a person you are interviewing is being treated.

> **SPECIAL NOTE:** Do not jump to too many conclusions based solely upon the medication history. Several of these medications also have nonpsychiatric uses.

Antianxiety Agents

Atarax (hydroxyzine)
Ativan (lorazepam)
Azene (clorazepate)
Buspar (buspirone)
Centrax (prazepam)
Equanil (meprobamate)
Librax (chlordiazepoxide)
Libritabs (chlordiazepoxide)
Librium (chlordiazepoxide)

Miltown (meprobamate)
Paxipam (halazepam)
Serax (oxazepam)
Tranxene (clorazepate)
Valium (diazepam)
Vestran (prazepam)
Vistaril (hydroxyzine)
Xanax (alprazolam)

Antidepressants

Adapin (doxepin)
Anafranil (clomipramine)
Asendin (amoxapine)
Aventyl (nortriptyline)

Norpramin (desipramine)
Pamelor (nortriptyline)
Parnate (tranylcypromine)
Paxil (paroxetine)

Antidepressants *(Continued)*

Desyrel (trazodone)
Effexor (venlafaxine)
Elavil (amitriptyline)
Endep (amitriptyline)
Etrafon (perphenazine
  & amitriptyline)
Limbitrol (chlordiazepoxide
  & amitriptyline)
Ludiomil (maprotiline)
Marplan (isocarboxazid)
Nardil (phenelzine)

Pertofrane (desipramine)
Prozac (fluoxetine)
Sinequan (doxepin)
Surmontil (trimipramine)
Tofranil (imipramine)
Triavil (perphenazine &
  amitriptyline)
Vivactil (protriptyline)
Wellbutrin (bupropion)
Zoloft (sertraline)

Antimanic Agents

Cibalith-s (lithium)
Depakote (divalproex)
Eskalith (lithium)

Lithane (lithium)
Lithium
Tegretol (carbamazepine)

Antiobsessional

Anafranil (clomipramine)

Antipsychotics

Clozaril (clozapine)
Compazine (prochlorperazine)
Daxolin (loxapine)
Haldol (haloperidol)
Lidone (molindone)
Loxitane (loxapine)
Mellaril (thioridazine)
Moban (molindone)
Navane (thiothixene)
Orap (pimozide)

Permitil (fluphenazine)
Prolixin (fluphenazine)
Risperdal (Risperidone)
Serentil (mesoridazine)
Stelazine (trifluoperazine)
Taractan (chlorprothixene)
Thorazine (chlorpromazine)
Trilafon (perphenazine)
Vesprin (triflupromazine)

Antispasmodics/Anticholinergics
(used for side-effects of the antipsychotics)

Akineton (biperiden)
Artane (trihexyphenidyl)
Benadryl (diphenhydramine)

Cogentin (benztropine)
Inderal (propranolol)
Symmetrel (amantadine)

Central Nervous System Stimulants
(used for hyperactivity)

Cylert (pemoline)   Ritalin (methylphenidate)
Dexedrine (dextroamphetamine)

Sedatives/Hypnotics
(used for sleep and seizure disorders)

Ambien (zolpidem tartrate)   Mebaral (mephobarbital)
Butisol (butabarbital)   Nembutal (pentobarbital)
Dalmane (flurazepam)   Noludar (methyprylon)
Depakene (valproic acid)   Phenobarbital
Depakote (divalproex)   Placidyl (ethchlorvynol)
Doral (quazepam)   ProSom (estazolam)
Halcion (triazolam)   Restoril (temazepam)
Klonopin (clonazepam)   Tegretol (carbamazepine)
                                 Valmid (ethinamate)

Miscellaneous

Antabuse   Revia (naltrexone)
  (curb alcohol abuse)   (curb alcohol abuse)
Methadone
  (substitute for heroin)

Appendix B

CASE STUDY—
MORGUE OPERATIONS

During the final preparation of this book, two air disasters focused attention upon the complexities of relief work with the professionals and the volunteers who assist with the difficult tasks of recovering and identifying the remains of those who lost their lives. Both of those 1994 accidents killed all passengers and crew on board and did so with such force upon impact that the planes and the bodies were blown apart and spread over large areas of ground. The recovery operations required workers to spend days combing the crash sites, cataloging the bits of the planes, the personal effects, and the human tissue that they found. From the sites, the victims' remains were taken to temporary morgues to begin the tedious process of identification.

As a DMH volunteer with ARC, I was asked to serve as Coordinator of DMH services at the morgue for the crash of USAir Flight 427-0908, which killed 132 persons near Pittsburgh, Pennsylvania. The morgue was set up in a hanger at an Air Force reserve base on the grounds of the airport. Another nearby hanger served as our primary staging and break areas. Throughout the 5-day assignment, I worked closely with a psychologist from the reserve unit and with other key command staff members to develop a standard operating procedure which can easily be transferred to other, similar situations.

MORGUE OPERATIONS

For anyone who is not familiar with a large, temporary morgue operation, it may be useful to briefly describe how they are set up. In addition to using pathologists, a large morgue includes specialists in fields such as fingerprinting, radiology, photography, dentistry, anthropology, and mortuary science. Experts from the FBI, state and local police, the coroners' offices in the region, and various teaching hospitals are usually present. Along with all the professionals are the members of their support staff. Many students preparing for careers in the related fields are also present. At this operation there was a staff of over 100 professionals on the job at any given time.

Representatives of the reserve unit were a key part of the team. Many served as organizers and trainers who briefed the newly assigned professionals and volunteers, helped suit them up, and then orchestrated their work as part of the team. Still other reservists served as security guards to maintain the confidentiality and privacy needed until identifications had been made.

A critical part of any large morgue operation is the group of volunteer *trackers*. These persons, many of whom were also reservists, are assigned to escort a body through the identification process. Here, they frequently were escorting small portions of decaying tissue and/or body parts, rather than large, easily recognizable whole bodies. They worked in 4-hour shifts, 1 per day, and tended to return day after day. Because most trackers had no medical backgrounds or prior exposures to anything like this, we made them our number-one priority.

Family members of the victims were not present at the morgue. The fact that they were being handled elsewhere (and kept away from the morgue) was something of a blessing for those persons working at the morgue, as their presence would have greatly heightened stress levels.

START-UP

The ARC DMH officer gave arriving volunteers a brief orientation to the operation when we arrived at our hotel. Upon arrival at the morgue, I met with my contacts from the reserve base. They fully briefed me on the morgue operation, and I was given a tour. I then spent about 90 minutes in the morgue, talking to professional workers and volunteer trackers who had begun working there in the days before my arrival. I was observing the process, using the time to assess any environmental mental health risks. It was an incredibly professional group of people who were working very hard to complete their difficult task. There were no signs of gallows humor, or of anything else that would detract from the serious nature of the work.

While inside, I noted several things that would likely become triggers for later memories. Vicks was being used in the face masks to help avoid the smells of decaying tissue and formaldehyde, forever changing the pleasant memories many had of mom using that on them when they had colds. Cafeteria trays were being used to carry bags containing small body parts. People inside were having trouble coping with any part of their jobs that put them in contact with personal effects. Whatever emotional distance and/or psychological defenses one had in place to help cope with the stress tended to fall away rather quickly when a photo or any similar identifying item was viewed. It suddenly made things too personal and led to thoughts and associations with one's own life ("That could have been my child") or with the strikingly detailed press accounts of the victims ("That was the couple I read about and saw profiled on TV").

Trackers assigned to the personal effects table, to go through luggage, were at especially high risk. We eventually eliminated that assignment, turning the job back over to members of the coroner's staff. Another high-risk spot was the photography table. Trackers there needed to manipulate the body parts so that the photographers could get their shots from various angles without having to constantly take gloves on and off before putting their cameras to their faces.

PRE-BRIEFING

Once recruited, trackers arrived 1 hour before their shifts began. They were given a group briefing by reservists who were in charge. The first 30 minutes offered a general overview of the morgue layout and operation, the various professional assignments, the many roles and responsibilities of trackers, and an explanation of gowning and universal precautions. The remainder of the briefing was done by my psychologist partner from the reserve unit and me. The main points of our 10 to 15 minute presentation were designed to:

1. Reinforce the graphic nature of the assignment, alerting them to the sights, sounds, smells, and potential psychological risks of the job (particularly when it came to dealings with personal effects and the photography area).
2. Elicit any questions on any aspect of the briefing that might need to be answered before they began.
3. Recommend they take breaks, both for fluid replenishment and emotional relief.
4. Describe to them the supports that were available during their shift—we had a few people circulating inside the morgue (to talk with professionals and trackers during any down time), and we had others available in the break areas.
5. Encourage use of a buddy-system, for peer support both now and after shifts ended.
6. Explain a requirement that all first-timers attend a brief group defusing session after their shifts (we also recommended and encouraged everyone to attend these sessions after every shift they worked); we made individual sessions available, too, for anyone uncomfortable with being part of a group.

Most important, perhaps, was our making a final plea to anyone who now felt this was not for them, to excuse himself or herself at any point in the process and come to see one of us. We also told them how special they all were for even considering to do this difficult work, and we thanked them for coming to help.

The pre-briefing was our way of doing stress inoculation. We tended to paint a graphic picture at this point, to serve as a stark reminder of the inherent emotional danger, and to be a final warning, similar to the signs one sees before boarding the major rides at a theme park. Still, no one withdrew at this point. Several folks did withdraw during or after shifts, but this was after the cumulative stress of re-exposure to the job had begun to appear. Many of those folks still wanted to stay with the job, and they did so after taking a day off or doing a less stressful assignment for 1 or 2 days.

DEFUSING

After each shift ended, the group of trackers (and anyone else from the morgue who was interested) joined us for a defusing session. We very briefly went through the same steps one would use for a debriefing: establishing basic ground rules; reviewing facts (sights, sounds, smells, and description of roles/ functions); discussing feelings and reactions/symptoms; teaching; and doing a wrap-up that made plans for any future actions and support mechanisms.

When a group (or individual) was hesitant to speak, an ice breaker was sometimes used to draw reactions from the group. Making a comment about how this use of Vicks would forever change a soothing childhood memory, or that they would probably never look at cafeteria trays in the same way, was usually enough to get things rolling. Not everyone would speak but those who did not talk could be seen nodding in affirmation as others made comments. Although we may have only spent a few minutes in each content area (other than the psychoeducation component), the time spent seemed to be enough to reassure everyone that their reactions were common and "normal." In the teaching phase, we spent a little extra time.

We usually began the teaching phase by answering any specific questions and dispelling any myths about the morgue process. Common concerns were things like, "Why did they sometimes have to crack (break) fingers to get finger prints?" (if the hand was clenched, fingers needed to be straightened in order to work with them) and "Why did they shoot pictures and videotape of the whole room one day?" (a record was being made for use in training those who might have to do this in the future). These kinds of issues raised concerns in the helpers about violation and invasion of privacy.

We then went on to discuss how their assignment might lead to one or more of the following reactions:

1. Normal daily routines may seem trivial and annoying for a while.
2. Workers may be physically and mentally tired despite little physical exertion.

3. They may alternate in and out of an interest in answering questions or discussing their experiences with family and friends (sometimes finding it helpful and other times finding it upsetting).
4. They may be sensitive about daily press reports or to seeing or reading about related incidents, real or dramatized, for some time to come (we urged many to avoid the media accounts altogether until some time had passed).
5. Exposure to any sights, sounds, or smells that are similar to those they just experienced might prompt recall of negative memories and related feelings.
6. Many might experience temporary changes in mood, loss of appetite, and/or sleep difficulties.
7. Family members may have trouble relating to the experience and handling any issues or changes it has prompted.
8. Anniversary reactions are likely to occur when the media gets going on extensive "1-year after" coverage (or reports on lawsuits, dedication of a memorial, etc.).

There were lots of questions in many sessions about how to discuss the accident and the morgue experience with children. That was no surprise, given lots of the trackers were heavily involved in flying, either as Air Force reservists or as members of families that were somehow related to persons in the airline industry. We had to help them confront some very real safety fears that are ordinarily kept out of routine family conversations. We distributed several ARC pamphlets and constantly needed to give hints on how to openly discuss tough issues and provide reassurance. We also distributed stress management brochures and material on how to make the transition from being a relief worker to handling day-to-day life tasks.

We could see changes in several of those who volunteered, especially those who returned day after day. Lots of returning volunteers were telling us of an inner strength and a drive to continue to do all they could, to help conclude the operation as quickly as possible. They wanted to help the victims' families have closure. We talked with them about the periods of reflection they were experiencing, and we told them that many life plans have been changed to include future disaster relief work, following receipt of the "calling" an incident of this type can provide.

At the end of the defusing, we urged everyone to take advantage of a longer, formal debriefing session; several were being planned to be held in the community when the job was done. We made a point of again thanking everyone for helping, and we shook their hands as they exited, to reinforce how special it was to tackle something few others would consider doing. One of us always stayed in the room until everyone else had left, because those needing special attention often remained behind to talk privately for a few moments.

OTHER CONSIDERATIONS

I have always been able to dress very casually for previous disaster assignments. This time I took dress shirts, slacks, and ties, and I was very glad I had done so. It seemed to be the most appropriate way to dress, given my need to work with professionals from a variety of fields, in the solemn mood that existed throughout the area.

Individual interventions during breaks and mealtime were usually short and off the subject of work. This was especially true for the many professionals who were working long hours in the morgue and were taking few breaks. Workers wanted to turn their attention away from the serious tasks they were doing. Once the presence of DMH workers was established, people could seek us out as they needed to do so. We had to be careful not to be too invasive of their private time. This assignment required a very low-key approach — patience and sensitivity were paramount.

There were many local DMH volunteers (new recruits) helping staff the morgue. They were rotating in and out at every 4-hour shift. Veteran workers had to orient them and caution them to tread lightly. None of the morgue workers or volunteers seemed to appreciate overly zealous mental health workers walking right up to them and asking, "How do you feel?" (or any similarly direct psychiatric interview questions). One must also be careful to avoid having too many DMH people in a sensitive area like a morgue because the sheer numbers will scare the workers; they may think we expect horrible things to happen and we will need so many of our people.

Another key point to stress is the extreme intensity of a morgue assignment. Several of us spent five 12-hour days at the morgue. While there, we tried to take frequent breaks, making it a day comparable to those I have done in earlier operations, where I had stayed more than twice as long. Still, I felt more tired following completion of my time on this assignment. Our local team sent five members to this job, and the others reported similar levels of tiredness at the end. This points up the need for good self-care and for workers to watch out for each other.

This was the first time I had traveled and worked with anyone from our local team, and it assured even stronger peer support than might have otherwise been possible. Prior to coming out to replace us, one member of our local team began calling those of us who were out, in order to provide support and check how we were doing each evening. That, too, allowed us additional opportunities to defuse, and it helped him become oriented to the job and his future role, prior to his arrival. We found both the buddy-system travel and the calls from home to be very helpful, and we plan to try to use them in future, in similar, high-stress situations.

If you find yourself needing to staff a morgue area, I would suggest that only experienced workers be used, and that they be volunteers who have been pre-screened, have been fully briefed, and have accepted the specific duties to which they will be assigned. Anyone who is new to DMH, or who is unsure of his or her tolerance levels for the kinds of intense experiences morgue work will yield, will likely need even more supervisory attention and peer support than seasoned workers, if placed in this environment. We do not want to create additional work for ourselves by exposing our own workers to emotional trauma and having them become psychological casualties.

Earlier in the book, I mentioned some things about how my wife has reacted to my volunteer work with the Red Cross. Each time I have a new experience with ARC, I learn a bit more about how she really feels about it and how well we do or do not know each other. When I was asked to go out on this assignment, it was obviously not her typical reaction. She was genuinely surprised I would even consider going to a morgue, questioning if I could handle it and finding the thought of my being there (or wanting to go there) to be extremely distasteful. Some of my coworkers and other family members had the same early reactions. In retrospect, it appears my family members and friends were struggling with some concerns and fears for my physical and psychological safety. They may also have been questioning if they could handle it themselves if they had been in my place. Those early reactions, and how bothersome this situation initially was in my wife's mind, serve as yet another reminder of how different a morgue assignment can be.

Clearly, working in or around a temporary morgue (or working with a recovery team at a crash site) is not the kind of assignment all DMH workers will want to handle. Despite the cautions I have provided, I must admit that I will take a similar assignment in the future if asked to do so. As with all of my previous assignments, I found myself doing things that were very helpful for others and, at the same time, professionally and emotionally rewarding for me.

REFERENCES

Abueg, F. R., Drescher, K. D., & Kubany, E. S. (1994). Natural disasters. In F. M. Dattilio & A. Freeman (Eds.), *Cognitive-Behavioral Approaches to Crisis Intervention* (pp. 238-257). New York: Guilford.

Ahearn, F. L., Jr., & Cohen, R. E. (1984). *Disasters and Mental Health: An Annotated Bibliography* (DHHS Publication No. ADM 84-1311). Rockville, MD: Center for Mental Health Services (formerly National Institute of Mental Health).

American Red Cross. (1987, May). *The Disaster Services Human Resources System Member's Handbook* (ARC 4419). Washington, DC: Author.

American Red Cross. (1991). *Coping With Disaster: Returning Home from a Disaster Assignment* (ARC 4473). Washington, DC: Author.

American Red Cross. (1994). *You Do What You Have to Do — Stories from the Great Flood of '93* (Videotape Stock No. A5031). Washington, DC: Author.

Armstrong, K. R., Lund, P. E., McWright, L. T., & Tichenor, V. (1995). Multiple stressor debriefing and the American Red Cross: The East Bay Hills fire experience. *Social Work, 40,* 83-90.

Barr, L. (1993, July 31). In the banks: The flood of '93 is history but work is just beginning. *Quad-City Times,* p. 1A.

Bartone, P. T., Ursano, R. J., Wright, K. M., & Ingraham, L. H. (1989). The impact of a military air disaster on the health of assistance workers: A prospective study. *The Journal of Nervous and Mental Disease, 177,* 317-328.

Baum, A., & Davidson, L. (1985). A suggested framework for studying factors that contribute to trauma in disaster. In B. J. Sowder (Ed.), *Disasters and Mental Health: Selected Contemporary Perspectives* (DHHS Publication No. ADM 85-1421, pp. 29-40). Rockville, MD: CMHS (formerly NIMH).

Beck, A. T. (1978). *Depression Inventory.* Philadelphia: Center for Cognitive Therapy.

Bille, D. A. (1993). Road to recovery: Post-traumatic stress disorder—The hidden victim. *Journal of Psychosocial Nursing, 31,* 19-28.

Bloom, B. L. (1985). *Stressful Life Event Theory and Research: Implications for Primary Prevention* (DHHS Publication No. ADM 85-1385). Rockville, MD: CMHS (formerly NIMH).

Bolin, R. (1985). Disaster characteristics and psychosocial impacts. In B. J. Sowder (Ed.), *Disasters and Mental Health: Selected Contemporary Perspectives* (DHHS Publication No. ADM 85-1421, pp. 3-28). Rockville, MD: CMHS (formerly NIMH).

Butcher, J. N., & Hatcher, C. (1988). The neglected entity in air disaster planning: Psychological services. *American Psychologist, 43,* 724-729.

Cannon, W. B. (1929). *Bodily Changes in Pain, Hunger, Fear and Rage.* New York: Appleton.

Carson, R. C., & Butcher, J. N. (1992). *Abnormal Psychology and Modern Life* (9th ed.). New York: Harper Collins.

Clark, M., & Friedman, D. (1992). Pulling together: Building a community debriefing team. *Journal of Psychosocial Nursing, 30,* 27-32.

Dattilio, F. M., & Freeman, A. (Eds.). (1994). *Cognitive-Behavioral Strategies in Crisis Intervention.* New York: Guilford.

Devine, E. T. (1904). *The Principles of Relief.* New York: Macmillan.

Devine, E. T. (1939). *When Social Work Was Young.* New York: Macmillan.

Farberow, N. L. (1978a). *Field Manual for Human Service Workers in Major Disasters* (DHHS Publication No. ADM 78-537). Rockville, MD: CMHS (formerly NIMH).

Farberow, N. L. (1978b). *Human Problems in Disasters: A Pamphlet for Government Emergency Disaster Services Personnel* (DHHS Publication No. ADM 78-539). Rockville, MD: CMHS (formerly NIMH).

Farberow, N. L. (1978c). *The Media in a Disaster* (DHHS Publication No. ADM 78-540). Rockville, MD: CMHS (formerly NIMH).

Farberow, N. L. (1978d). *Training Manual for Human Service Workers in Major Disasters* (DHHS Publication No. ADM 83-538). Rockville, MD: CMHS (formerly NIMH).

Farberow, N. L., & Gordon, N. S. (1981). *Manual for Child Health Workers in Major Disasters* (DHHS Publication No. ADM 81-1070). Rockville, MD: CMHS (formerly NIMH).

Federal Emergency Management Agency (FEMA). (1981). *The Effects of Cultural Difference on Face-to-Face Relationships Between Disaster Victims and Disaster Workers.* Washington, DC: Author

Flynn, B. (1987). Returning home following disaster work. In *Prevention and Control of Stress Among Emergency Workers: A Pamphlet for Team Managers* (DHHS Publication No. ADM 90-1497, pp. 6-9). Rockville, MD: CMHS (formerly NIMH).

Frederick, C. J. (Ed.). (1981). *Aircraft Accidents: Emergency Mental Health Problems* (DHHS Publication No. ADM 81-956). Rockville, MD: CMHS (formerly NIMH).

Freedman, A. M., Kaplan, H. I., & Sadock, B. J. (1972). *Modern Synopsis of Comprehensive Textbook of Psychiatry.* Baltimore: Williams & Wilkins.

Friedman, P., & Linn, L. (1957). Some psychiatric notes on the Andrea Doria disaster. *American Journal of Psychiatry, 114,* 426-432.

Garrison, W. (1986). Neuro-linguistic programming: An optional intervention to post traumatic incident counseling. In J. T. Reese & H. A. Goldstein (Eds.), *Psychological Services for Law Enforcement* (pp. 351-355). Washington, DC: Department of Justice.

Garrison, W., Reese, E., & Reese, M. (1993, November). *After the Storm . . . After the Trauma.* Seminar presented at the National Association of Social Workers Annual Meeting, Orlando, FL.

Hartsough, D. M. (1985). Stress and mental health interventions in three major disasters. In D. M. Hartsough & D. G. Myers (Eds.), *Disaster Work and Mental Health: Prevention and Control of Stress Among Workers* (DHHS Publication No. ADM 85-1422, pp. 1-44). Rockville, MD: CMHS (formerly NIMH).

Heffron, E. F. (1977). Project outreach: Crisis intervention following natural disaster. *Journal of Community Psychology, 5,* 103-111.

Holmes, T. H., & Rahe, R. H. (1967). The social readjustment rating scale. *Journal of Psychosomatic Research, 11,* 213-218.

Jacobs, G. A., Quevillon, R. P., & Stricherz, M. (1990). Lessons from the aftermath of flight 232: Practical considerations for the mental health profession's response to air disasters. *American Psychologist, 45,* 1329-1335.

Janis, I. L. (1958). *Psychological Stress: Psychoanalytic and Behavioral Studies of Surgical Patients.* New York: Wiley.

Jones, D. R. (1985). Secondary Disaster Victims: The Emotional Effects of Recovering and Identifying Human Remains. *American Journal of Psychiatry, 142,* 303-307.

Jordan, C. (1976). Pastoral care and chronic disaster victims: The Buffalo Creek experience. *The Journal of Pastoral Care, 30,* 159-170.

Kadushin, A. (1976). *Supervision in Social Work.* New York: Columbia University Press.

Kafrissen, S. R., Heffron, E. F., & Zusman, J. (1975). Mental health problems in environmental disasters. In H. L. P. Resnik, H. L. Ruben, & D. D. Ruben (Eds.), *Emergency Psychiatric Care: The Management of Mental Health Crises* (pp. 157-170). Bowie, MD: The Charles Press.

Kindler, J., Duncan, J., & Knapp, S. (1991). The process of helping. *The Pennsylvania Psychologist, 51,* 15-17.

Kubler-Ross, E. (1969). *On Death and Dying.* New York: Macmillan.

Lee, K., Furukawa, P., Malinoski, G., Kaplan, K., & Furuto, S. (1993, November). *Between Crisis and Chronicity: The Crucial Phase of Disaster Response.* Workshop presented at the National Association of Social Workers Annual Meeting, Orlando, FL.

Lifton, R. J., & Olson, E. (1976). Death imprint in Buffalo Creek. In H. J. Parad, H. L. P. Resnik, & L. G. Parad (Eds.), *Emergency and Disaster Management: A Mental Health Sourcebook* (pp. 295-308). Bowie, MD: The Charles Press.

Lindemann, E. (1944). Symptomatology and management of acute grief. *American Journal of Psychiatry, 101,* 141-148.

Lindy, J. D., & Grace, M. (1985). The recovery environment: Continuing stressor versus a healing psychosocial space. In B. J. Sowder (Ed.), *Disasters and Mental Health: Selected Contemporary Perspectives* (DHHS Publication No. ADM 85-1421, pp. 137-149). Rockville, MD: CMHS (formerly NIMH).

Lystad, M. (Ed.). (1985). *Innovations in Mental Health Services to Disaster Victims* (DHHS Publication No. ADM 85-1390). Rockville, MD: CMHS (formerly NIMH).

Mannino, F. V., MacLennan, B. W., & Shore, M. F. (1975). *The Practice of Mental Health Consultation* (DHHS Publication No. ADM 74-112). Rockville, MD: CMHS (formerly NIMH).

Mannino, F. V., Trickett, E. J., Shore, M. F., Kidder, M. G., & Levin, G. (Eds.). (1986). *Handbook of Mental Health Consultation* (DHHS Publication No. ADM 86-1446). Rockville, MD: CMHS (formerly NIMH).

Mays, R. A., Jr. (Panel Leader). (1993, November). *Natural Disasters and Humanitarian Operations: The Federal Social Work Response.* Workshop presented at the National Association of Social Workers Annual Meeting, Orlando, FL.

McClung, F. B., & Stunden, A. A. (1972). *Mental Health Consultation to Programs for Children* (DHHS Publication No. ADM 72-9088). Rockville, MD: CMHS (formerly NIMH).

Meichenbaum, D. (1985). *Stress Inoculation Training.* New York: Pergamon.

Mitchell, J. T. (1983, January). When disaster strikes . . . The critical incident stress debriefing process. *Journal of Emergency Services, 8,* 36-39.

Mitchell, J. T. (1988, November). Stress: The history, status and future of critical incident stress debriefings. *Journal of Emergency Services, 13,* 47-52.

Myers, D. G. (1985). Helping the helpers: A training manual. In D. M. Hartsough & D. G. Myers (Eds.), *Disaster Work and Mental Health: Prevention and Control of Stress Among Workers* (DHHS Publication No. ADM 85-1422, pp. 45-149). Rockville, MD: CMHS (formerly NIMH).

Myers, D. G. (1994). *Disaster Response and Recovery: A Handbook for Mental Health Professionals* (DHHS Publication No. SMA 94-3010). Rockville, MD: CMHS (formerly NIMH).

National Institute of Mental Health. (1985). *Role Stressors and Supports for Emergency Workers* (DHHS Publication No. ADM 90-1408). Rockville, MD: Author (now known as CMHS).

National Institute of Mental Health. (1988a). *Prevention and Control of Stress Among Emergency Workers: A Pamphlet for Team Managers* (DHHS Publication No. ADM 88-1496). Rockville, MD: Author (now known as CMHS).

National Institute of Mental Health. (1988b). *Prevention and Control of Stress Among Emergency Workers: A Pamphlet for Workers* (DHHS Publication No. ADM 88-1497). Rockville, MD: Author (now known as CMHS).

Nolen-Hoeksema, S., & Morrow, J. (1991). A prospective study of depression and posttraumatic stress symptoms after a natural disaster: The 1989 Loma Prieta earthquake. *Journal of Personality and Social Psychology, 61,* 115-121.

Osterweis, M., & Townsend, J. (1988a). *Health Professionals and the Bereaved* (DHHS Publication No. ADM 88-1552). Rockville, MD: CMHS (formerly NIMH).

Osterweis, M., & Townsend, J. (1988b). *Mental Health Professionals and the Bereaved* (DHHS Publication No. ADM 88-1554). Rockville, MD: CMHS (formerly NIMH).

Parad, H. J., & Resnik, H. L. P. (1975b). The practice of crisis intervention in emergency care. In H. L. P. Resnik, H. L. Ruben, & D. D. Ruben (Eds.), *Emergency Psychiatric Care: The Management of Mental Health Crises* (pp. 23-34). Bowie, MD: The Charles Press.

Parad, H. J., Resnik, H. L. P., Ruben, H. L., Zusman, J., & Ruben, D. D. (1975a). Crisis intervention and emergency health care: Concepts and principles. In H. L. P. Resnik, H. L. Ruben, & D. D. Ruben (Eds.), *Emergency Psychiatric Care: The Management of Mental Health Crises* (pp. 1-21). Bowie, MD: The Charles Press.

Price, R. (1993, August 6). Tales of triumph, tragedy. *USA TODAY,* p. 3A.

Quarantelli, E. L. (1985). What is disaster? The need for clarification in definition and conceptualization in research. In B. J. Sowder (Ed.), *Disasters and Mental Health: Selected Contemporary Perspectives* (DHHS Publication No. ADM 85-1421, pp. 41-73). Rockville, MD: CMHS (formerly NIMH).

Quevillon, R. P., & Jacobs, G. A. (1992). Treatment issues in mental health responses to disasters. In L. VandeCreek, S. Knapp, & T. L. Jackson (Eds.), *Innovations in Clinical Practice: A Source Book* (Vol. 11, pp. 403-411). Sarasota, FL: Professional Resource Press.

Resnik, H. L. P., Ruben, H. L., & D. D. Ruben (Eds.). (1975). *Emergency Psychiatric Care: The Management of Mental Health Crises.* Bowie, MD: The Charles Press.

Ritter, J. (1993, August 5). The victims. *USA Today*, p. 8A.

Robinson, R. C., & Mitchell, J. T. (1993). Evaluation of psychological debriefings. *Journal of Traumatic Stress, 6*, 367-382.

Seligman, M. (1975). *Helplessness: On Depression, Development, and Death*. San Francisco: W. H. Freeman.

Seyle, H. (1956). *The Stress of Life*. New York: McGraw-Hill.

Sherwood, R. J. (1991). Vietnam veterans: A hidden population in social work practice. *Journal of Independent Social Work, 5*, 7-17.

Siporin, M. (1987). Disasters and disaster aid. In *Encyclopedia of Social Work* (18th ed., pp. 438-449). Silver Springs, MD: National Association of Social Workers.

Solomon, S. D., & Green, B. L. (1992, Winter). Mental health effects of natural and human-made disasters. *PTSD Research Quarterly, 3*, 1-7.

Sowder, B. J. (Ed.). (1985). *Disasters and Mental Health: Selected Contemporary Perspectives* (DHHS Publication No. ADM 85-1421). Rockville, MD: CMHS (formerly NIMH).

Talbot, A. (1990). The importance of parallel process in debriefing crisis counsellors. *Journal of Traumatic Stress, 3*, 265-277.

Tecala, M. R. (1993, November). *PTSD: Causes, Symptoms, and Treatment*. Workshop presented at the National Association of Social Workers Annual Meeting, Orlando, FL.

Tierney, K. J., & Baisden, B. (1979). *Crisis Intervention Programs for Disaster Victims: A Source Book and Manual for Smaller Communities* (DHHS Publication No. ADM 83-675). Rockville, MD: CMHS (formerly NIMH).

Titchener, J. L., Kapp, F. T., & Winget, C. (1976). The Buffalo Creek syndrome: Symptoms and character change after a major disaster. In H. J. Parad, H. L. P. Resnik, & L. G. Parad (Eds.), *Emergency and Disaster Management: A Mental Health Sourcebook* (pp. 283-294). Bowie, MD: The Charles Press.

U.S. General Accounting Office. (1993, July 23). *Disaster Management: Improving the Nation's Response to Catastrophic Disasters* (Washington, DC: GAO/RCED-93-186).

Ward, S. (1993, August 5). When the guard is called. *USA Today*, p. 1A.

Weaver, J. D. (1984). Work-related stressors and means of coping among crisis intervention workers and their spouses. *Emotional First Aid: A Journal of Crisis Intervention, 1*, 14-24.

Weaver, J. D. (1993a). Chapter embarks on partnership with American Red Cross. *The Pennsylvania Social Worker, 14,* 3.

Weaver, J. D. (1993b). *An Untapped Resource: Working With Volunteers Who Are Mentally Ill.* Walla Walla, WA: MacDuff Bunt Associates (MBA).

Weiss, R. S. (1987). Recovery from bereavement: Findings and issues. In J. A. Steinberg & M. M. Silverman (Eds.), *Preventing Mental Disorders: A Research Perspective* (pp. 108-121). Rockville, MD: CMHS (formerly NIMH).

Williams, C. L., Solomon, S. D., & Bartone, P. (1988). Primary prevention in aircraft disasters: Integrating research and practice. *American Psychologist, 43,* 730-739.

Zarle, T., Hartsough, D., & Ottinger, D. (1974). Tornado recovery: The development of a professional-paraprofessional response to a disaster. *Journal of Community Psychology, 4,* 311-321.

INDEX

R

S

American Red Cross

Although officially chartered by Congress in 1904 to provide disaster relief, the American Red Cross has, in fact, been providing help to survivors of disasters for well over a hundred years. Each year Red Cross workers respond to about 60,000 disasters.

In addition to supplying care and aid following disasters, the Red Cross also provides free information to help people to plan for potential disasters, reduce their traumatic impact, prevent injuries, save lives, and reduce the loss of property.

How You Can Help . . .

If you would like to make a contribution to the American Red Cross general disaster fund or to aid victims of a specific disaster, please send checks, money orders, or credit card information to the address below. Credit card donations can also be accepted by calling our 800 numbers.

Disaster Relief Fund
American Red Cross
P.O. Box 37243
Washington, DC 20013

1-800-842-2200 (English)
1-800-257-7575 (Spanish)

Add A Colleague To Our Mailing List . . .

If you would like us to send our latest catalog to one of your colleagues, please return this form.

Name:_____

(Please Print)

Address:_____

Address:_____

City/State/Zip:_____

Telephone:(_____)_____

I am a:

_____ Psychologist
_____ Psychiatrist
_____ School Psychologist
_____ Clinical Social Worker

_____ Mental Health Counselor
_____ Marriage and Family Therapist
_____ Not in Mental Health Field
_____ Other:_____

◆　　　◆　　　◆

Professional Resource Press
P.O. Box 15560
Sarasota, FL 34277-1560

Telephone #813-366-7913
FAX #813-366-7971

If You Found This Book Useful . . .

You might want to know more about our other titles.

If you would like to receive our latest catalog, please return this form:

Name:_____

(Please Print)

Address:_____

Address:_____

City/State/Zip:_____

Telephone:(_____)_____

I am a:

_____ Psychologist   _____ Mental Health Counselor
_____ Psychiatrist   _____ Marriage and Family Therapist
_____ School Psychologist   _____ Not in Mental Health Field
_____ Clinical Social Worker _____ Other:_____

◆   ◆   ◆

Professional Resource Press
P.O. Box 15560
Sarasota, FL 34277-1560

Telephone #813-366-7913
FAX #813-366-7971